Masculine Domination

Masculine Domination

Pierre Bourdieu

Translated by Richard Nice

Stanford University Press
Stanford, California

Stanford University Press
Stanford, California
© 1998 Editions du Seuil
This translation © 2001 Polity Press
First published in France as *La domination masculine* by Editions du Seuil
Originating publisher of English edition: Polity Press in association with
  Blackwell Publishers Ltd.
First published in the U.S.A. by Stanford University Press, 2001
Published with the assistance of the French Ministry of Culture

Cloth ISBN 0-8047-3818-1
Paper ISBN 0-8047-3820-3
Library of Congress Card Number: 2001-086078

This book is printed on acid-free paper.

Last figure below indicates year of this printing:
09

Contents

Preface to the English edition

Eternalizing the arbitrary

This book, in which I have taken the opportunity to clarify, support and correct my previous arguments on the same subject with the help of the many works devoted to the relations between the sexes, addresses *explicitly* a question that is obsessively raised by most commentators (and most of my critics) – that of (observed or desired) permanence or change in the sexual order. It is, indeed, the importation and imposition of this naive and naively normative opposition that leads people, against all the evidence, to see the conclusion reached as to the relative constancy of sexual structures and the schemes through which they are perceived as a way – immediately denounced and refuted with a reminder of all the changes that have occurred in the position of women – of denying and condemning those changes.

That question needs to be countered with another question, one that is scientifically more pertinent and, in my view, politically more urgent: if it is true that the relations between the sexes have changed less than superficial observation would suggest and that knowledge of the objective structures and cognitive structures of a particularly well-preserved androcentric society (such as Kabyle society, as I observed it in the early 1960s) provides instruments enabling one to understand some of the best concealed aspects of what those relations are in the economically most advanced societies, then one has to ask what are the *historical* mechanisms responsible for the *relative dehistoricization* and *eternalization* of the structure of the sexual division and the corresponding principles of division. Posing the question in those terms marks an advance in the order of knowledge which can be the basis of a decisive advance in the order of action. To point out that what appears, in history, as being eternal is merely the product of a labour of eternalization performed by interconnected institutions such as the family, the church, the state, the educational system, and also, in another order of things, sport and journalism (these abstract notions being simple shorthand markers for complex mechanisms which must be analysed in each case in their historical particularity) is to reinsert into history, and therefore to restore to historical action, the relationship between the sexes that the naturalistic and essentialist vision removes from them (and not, as some have claimed I have said, to try to stop history and to dispossess women of their role as historical agents).

Combating these historical forces of dehistoricization must be the most immediate objective of an enterprise of mobilization aimed at putting history in motion again by neutralizing the mechanisms of the neutralization of history. This strictly *political* mobilization, which would open for women the possibility of a collective action of resistance, oriented towards legal and political reforms, contrasts both with the resignation that is encouraged by all essentialist (biological or psychoanalytical) visions of the difference between the sexes and with a resistance that is reduced to individual acts or the endlessly recommenced discursive 'happenings' that are recommended by some feminist theoreticians – these heroic breaks in the everyday routine, such as the 'parodic performances' favoured by Judith Butler, probably expect too much for the meagre and uncertain results they obtain.

To call on women to engage in a political action that breaks with the temptation of the introverted revolt of small mutual support groups – however necessary these groups may be in the vicissitudes of everyday struggles, in the home, the factory or the office – does not mean, as one might think and fear, inviting them to subscribe without a struggle to the ordinary forms and norms of political struggle, at the risk of finding themselves annexed or swallowed up by movements alien to their own preoccupations and interests. It expresses the wish that they will work – within the social movement itself, and supported by the organizations that have sprung from the revolt against symbolic domination, of which, along with homosexuals, they are one of the main victims – to invent and impose forms of collective organization and action and effective weapons, especially symbolic ones, capable of shaking the political and legal institutions which play a part in perpetuating their subordination.

—— Prelude ——

I would probably not have embarked on such a difficult subject if I had not been compelled to do so by the whole logic of my research. I have always been astonished by what might be called the *paradox of doxa* – the fact that the order of the world as we find it, with its one-way streets and its no-entry signs, whether literal or figurative, its obligations and its penalties, is broadly respected; that there are not more transgressions and subversions, contraventions and 'follies' (just think of the extraordinary concordance of thousands of dispositions – or wills – implied in five minutes' movement of traffic around the Place de la Bastille or Place de la Concorde . . .); or, still more surprisingly, that the established order, with its relations of domination, its rights and prerogatives, privileges and injustices, ultimately perpetuates itself so easily, apart from a few historical accidents, and that the most intolerable conditions of existence can so often be perceived as acceptable and even natural. And I have also seen masculine domination, and the way it is imposed and suffered, as the prime example of this paradoxical submission, an effect of what I call symbolic violence, a gentle violence, imperceptible and invisible even to its victims,

I am not sure whether giving thanks by name would be a blessing or a curse for those concerned, and so I shall simply record here my deep gratitude to all those (men and especially women) who have supplied me with testimonies, documents, references and ideas; and my hope that, especially in its effects, this work will be worthy of the confidence and expectations they have placed in it.

exerted for the most part through the purely symbolic chan-
nels of communication and cognition (more precisely, misrecognition), recognition, or even feeling. This extraordinarily
ordinary social relation thus offers a privileged opportunity
to grasp the logic of the domination exerted in the name of a
symbolic principle known and recognized both by the dominant and by the dominated – a language (or a pronunciation),
a lifestyle (or a way of thinking, speaking and acting) – and,
more generally, a distinctive property, whether emblem or
stigma, the symbolically most powerful of which is that perfectly arbitrary and non-predictive bodily property, skin colour.

It is clear that in these areas one must above all restore the
paradoxical character of *doxa* while at the same time dismant-
ling the processes responsible for this transformation of history
into nature, of cultural arbitrariness into the *natural*. And to do
so, one has to adopt the point of view on our own world and
our own vision of the world which is that of the anthropolo-
gist, capable of showing that the principle of division (*nomos*)
which founds the difference between male and female as we
(mis)recognize it is simultaneously arbitrary, contingent, and
also socio-logically necessary. It is no accident that, when she
wants to suspend what she magnificently calls 'the hypnotic
power of domination', Virginia Woolf resorts to an ethnographic analogy, genetically relating the segregation of women
to the rituals of an archaic society: 'Inevitably, we look upon
societies as conspiracies that sink the private brother, whom
many of us have reason to respect, and inflate in his stead a
monstrous male, loud of voice, hard of fist, childishly intent
upon scoring the floor of the earth with chalk marks, within
whose mystic boundaries human beings are penned, rigidly, separately, artificially; where, daubed red and gold, decorated like
a savage with feathers, he goes through mystic rites and enjoys
the dubious pleasures of power and dominion while we, "his"
women, are locked in the private house without share in the
many societies of which his society is composed.'[1] 'Mystic
boundaries', 'mystic rites' – this language, the language of the
magical transformation and symbolic conversion produced by
ritual consecration, the basis of a new birth, is an invitation to

---

1   V. Woolf, *Three Guineas* (London: Hogarth Press, 1939), p. 121.

orient research towards an approach capable of grasping the specifically symbolic dimension of male domination.

And so one has to seek in a materialist analysis of the economy of symbolic goods the means of escaping from the ruinous choice between the 'material' and the 'spiritual' or 'ideal' [*idéel*] (perpetuated nowadays in the opposition between would-be 'materialist' studies which explain the asymmetry between the sexes in terms of the conditions of production and what are called 'symbolic' studies, which are often remarkable, but partial). But, before that, only a very particular use of ethnology can make it possible to carry out the project, suggested by Virginia Woolf, of scientifically objectifying the truly mystical operation of which the division between the sexes as we know it is the product, or, in other words, of treating the objective analysis of a society organized through and through according to the androcentric principle (the Kabyle tradition) as an objective archaeology of our unconscious, in other words as the instrument of a genuine socioanalysis.[2]

This detour through an exotic tradition is indispensable in order to break the relationship of deceptive familiarity that binds us to our own tradition. The biological appearances and the very real effects that have been produced in bodies and minds by a long collective labour of socialization of the biological and biologicization of the social combine to reverse the relationship between causes and effects and to make a naturalized social construction ('genders' as sexually characterized habitus) appear as the grounding in nature of the arbitrary division which underlies both reality and the representation of reality and which sometimes imposes itself even on scientific research.[3]

2   If only to show that my present intention does not stem from a recent conversion, I refer the reader to the pages of a book, written two decades ago, in which I insisted that, when applied to the sexual division of the world, ethnology can 'become a particularly powerful form of socio-analysis' (P. Bourdieu, *The Logic of Practice* (Cambridge: Polity, 1990, p. 14; French edition published in 1980).
3   Thus it is not uncommon for example for psychologists to take over the common vision of the sexes as radically separate sets, without intersections, and to ignore the degree of *overlap* between the distributions of male and female performances and the differences (of magnitude) between the differences observed in various domains (from sexual anatomy to intelligence). Or, worse, they often let themselves be guided, in *constructing* and *describing* their object, by the principles of vision and division embedded in ordinary

But does not this quasi-analytical use of ethnography to historicize and so denaturalize what seems most natural in the social order, the division between the sexes, run the risk of bringing to light constants and invariants – which are the very basis of its socioanalytical efficacy – and thereby of ratifying and eternalizing a conservative representation of the relationship between the sexes, the very one which is condensed in the myth of the 'eternal feminine'? Here one has to confront a new paradox, entailing a complete revolution in the approach to what researchers have aimed to study under the rubric of 'women's history': do not the invariants which, beyond all the visible changes in the position of women, are observed in the relations of domination between the sexes require one to take as one's privileged object the historical mechanisms and institutions which, in the course of history, have continuously abstracted these invariants from history?

This cognitive revolution would inevitably have consequences at the level of practice, and, in particular, in the formulation of strategies aimed at transforming the present state of the material and symbolic power relation between the sexes. If it is true that the principle of the perpetuation of this relationship of domination does not truly reside (or, at least, not principally) in one of the most visible sites in which it is exercised – in other words, within the domestic sphere, on which some feminist debate has concentrated its attention – but in agencies such as the school or the state, sites where principles of domination that go on to be exercised within even the most private universe are developed and imposed, then a vast field of action is opened up for feminist struggles, which are thus called upon to take a distinctive and decisive place within political struggles against *all* forms of domination.

---

language, either seeking to measure differences identified in that language – such as the more 'aggressive' nature of men or the more 'timid' nature of women – or using ordinary, and therefore value-laden, terms to describe those differences. See, as examples among many others, J. A. Sherman, *Sex-Related Cognitive Differences: An Essay on Theory and Evidence* (Springfield, Ill.: Thomas, 1978); M. B. Parlee, 'Psychology: review essay', *Signs: Journal of Women in Culture and Society*, 1 (1975), pp. 119–38 – especially on the balance-sheet of the mental and behavioural differences between the sexes drawn up by J. E. Garai and A. Scheinfeld in 1968; M. B. Parlee, 'The Premenstrual Syndrome', *Psychological Bulletin*, 80 (1973), pp. 454–65.

— 1 —

A magnified image

Being included, as man or woman, in the object that we are trying to comprehend, we have embodied the historical structures of the masculine order in the form of unconscious schemes of perception and appreciation. When we try to understand masculine domination we are therefore likely to resort to modes of thought that are the product of domination. Our only hope of breaking out of that circle lies in finding a practical strategy for objectifying the subject of scientific objectification. STRATEGY This strategy, the one I shall adopt here, consists in transforming an exercise of transcendental reflection aimed at exploring the 'categories of understanding' – or, in Durkheim's terms, the 'forms of classification' with which we construct the world (but which, as products of that world, are largely attuned to it, so that they remain unnoticed) – into a kind of laboratory experiment. This will consist in treating ethnographic analysis of the objective structures and cognitive forms of a particular historical society, at once exotic and very close to us, both strange and familiar, that of the Berbers of Kabylia, as the instrument of a socioanalysis of the androcentric unconscious that is capable of objectifying the categories of that unconscious.[1]

1 I would probably not have been able to appreciate the analysis of masculine perception contained in Virginia Woolf's *To the Lighthouse* (which I discuss below) if I had not reread it with an eye informed by the Kabyle vision (V. Woolf, *To the Lighthouse* (Harmondsworth: Penguin, 1964), p. 20).

Beyond the conquests and conversions they have undergone, and no doubt in reaction against them, the highland peasants of Kabylia have preserved structures which, protected in particular by the relatively unaltered practical coherence of behaviours and discourses partially abstracted from time by ritual stereotyping, represent a paradigmatic form of the 'phallonarcissistic' vision and the andro-centric cosmology which are common to all Mediterranean societies and which survive even today, but in a partial and, as it were, exploded state, in our own cognitive structures and social structures. The choice of the particular case of Kabylia is justified when one knows, on the one hand, that the cultural tradition that has been maintained there constitutes a paradigmatic realization of the Mediterranean tradition (this is readily confirmed by consulting the ethnological research devoted to the question of honour and shame in various Mediter-ranean societies – Greece, Italy, Spain, Egypt, Turkey, Kabylia, etc.);[2] and on the other hand, that the whole European cultural domain undeniably shares in that tradition, as is shown by a comparison of the rituals observed in Kabylia with those collected by Arnold Van Gennep in early twentieth-century France.[3] I could no doubt also have drawn on the tradition of ancient Greece, from which psychoanalysis has borrowed the greater part of its interpretative schemes, under-pinned by the substantial research done in the field of historical ethnography. But nothing can replace direct study of a still function-ing system that has remained relatively untouched by semi-learned reinterpretations (because of the lack of a written tradition). As I have indicated elsewhere,[4] analysis of a corpus like that of ancient Greece, whose production extends over several centuries, runs the risk of arti-ficially *synchronizing* successive and different states of the system and above all of conferring the same epistemological status on texts that have subjected the old mythico-ritual heritage to various more or less extensive reworkings. The interpreter who claims to act as an ethno-grapher is thus liable to treat as 'naive' informants authors who themselves were already acting as (quasi-) ethnographers and whose mythological evocations, even the seemingly most archaic ones, such as those of Homer or Hesiod, are already learned myths implying

2   Cf. J. Peristiany, *Honour and Shame: The Values of Mediterranean Society* (Chicago: University of Chicago Press, 1974), and J. Pitt-Rivers, *Mediterranean Countrymen: Essays in the Social Anthropology of the Mediterranean* (Paris and The Hague: Mouton, 1963).
3   A. Van Gennep, *Manuel de folklore français contemporain* (3 vols, Paris: Picard, 1937–58).
4   Cf. P. Bourdieu, 'Lecture, lecteurs, lettres, littérature', in *Choses dites* (Paris: Éditions de Minuit, 1987), pp. 132–43.

omissions, distortions and reinterpretations (and what can one say when, like Michel Foucault in the second volume of his *History of Sexuality*, a researcher chooses to start the survey of sexuality and the subject with Plato, ignoring authors like Homer, Hesiod, Aeschylus, Sophocles, Herodotus or Aristophanes, not to mention the pre-Socratic philosophers, in whom the old Mediterranean heritage is more clearly visible?). The same ambiguity is found in all would-be scientific works (especially medical ones), in which one cannot distinguish what is borrowed from authorities (such as Aristotle, who, on some essential points, himself converted the old Mediterranean mythology into learned myth) from what is reinvented from the structures of the unconscious and sanctioned or ratified by borrowed knowledge.

The social construction of bodies

In a universe in which, as in Kabyle society, the order of sexuality is not constituted as such and where sexual differences remain immersed in the set of oppositions that organize the whole cosmos, sexual attributes and acts are heavily charged with anthropological and cosmological determinations. There is thus a danger of misinterpreting their deep significance if one approaches them in terms of the category of the sexual in itself. The constitution of the sexual as such (which culminates in eroticism) has caused us to lose the sense of the sexualized cosmology that is rooted in a sexualized topology of the socialized body, of its movements and displacements which are immediately charged with social meaning – upward movement being, for example, associated with the male, through erection or the upper position in the sexual act.

The division of (sexual and other) things and activities according to the opposition between the male and the female, while arbitrary when taken in isolation, receives its objective and subjective necessity from its insertion into a system of homologous oppositions – up/down, above/below, in front/behind, right/left, straight/curved (and twisted), dry/wet, spicy/bland, light/dark, outside (public)/inside (private), etc. – which in some cases correspond to movements of the body (up/down // go up/go down // inside/outside // go in/come out). Being similar in difference, these oppositions are sufficiently concordant to support one other, in and through the inexhaustible play of practical transfers and metaphors, and sufficiently divergent to give each of them a kind of semantic thickness, resulting from overdetermination by harmonics, connotations and correspondences.[5]

These universally applicable schemes of thought record as differences of nature, inscribed in objectivity, variations and distinctive features (of physique, for example) which they help to make exist at the same time as they 'naturalize' them by inscribing them in a system of differences, all equally natural in appearance. As a result, the anticipations they engender are endlessly confirmed by the course of the world, in particular by all the biological and cosmic cycles. So it is not clear how the social relation of domination which underlies them and which, in a complete reversal of causes and effects, appears as one application among others of a system of sense relations perfectly independent of power relations, could emerge to consciousness. The mythico-ritual system here plays a role equivalent to that performed by the legal system in differentiated societies: in so far as the principles of vision and division that it proposes are objectively adjusted to the pre-existing divisions, it consecrates the established order, by bringing it to known and recognized, official existence.

The division between the sexes appears to be 'in the order of things', as people sometimes say to refer to what is normal, natural, to the point of being inevitable: it is present both – in the objectified state – in things (in the house, for example, every part of which is 'sexed'), in the whole social world, and – in the embodied state – in the habitus of the agents, functioning as systems of schemes of perception, thought and action. (Where, for the purposes of communication, I speak, as I do here, of categories or cognitive structures, at the risk of seeming to fall into the intellectualist philosophy that I have always criticized, it would be better to speak of practical schemes or dispositions: the word 'category' sometimes seems appropriate because it has the advantage of designating both a social unit – the category of farmers – and a cognitive

5 For a detailed table of the distribution of activities between the sexes, see P. Bourdieu, *The Logic of Practice* (Cambridge: Polity, 1990), p. 217.

structure and of showing the link between them.) It is the concordance between the objective structures and the cognitive structures, between the shape of being and the forms of knowledge, between the course of the world and expectations about it, that makes possible what Husserl described under the name of the 'natural attitude' or 'doxic experience' – but without pointing to its social conditions of possibility. This experience apprehends the social world and its arbitrary divisions, starting with the socially constructed division between the sexes, as natural, self-evident, and as such contains a full recognition of legitimacy. It is because they fail to observe the action of deep-rooted mechanisms, such as those which underlie the agreement between cognitive structures and social structures, and consequently the doxic experience of the social world (for example, in modern societies, the reproductive logic of the educational system) that thinkers with very different philosophical stances can attribute all the symbolic effects of legitimation (or sociodicy) to factors belonging to the order of more or less conscious and intentional *representation* ('ideology', 'discourse', etc.).

The strength of the masculine order is seen in the fact that it dispenses with justification:[6] the androcentric vision imposes itself as neutral and has no need to spell itself out in discourses aimed at legitimating it.[7] The social order functions as an immense symbolic machine tending to ratify the masculine domination on which it is founded: it is the sexual division of labour, a very strict distribution of the activities assigned to each sex, of their place, time and instruments; it is the structure of space, with the opposition between the place of assembly or the market, reserved for men, and the house, reserved for

6   It has often been observed that, both in social perception and in language, the masculine gender appears as non-marked, in a sense neuter, in opposition to the feminine, which is explicitly characterized. Dominique Merllié has been able to verify this in the case of recognition of the 'sex' of handwriting, where only female features are perceived as present or absent (cf. D. Merllié, 'Le sexe de l'écriture. Note sur la perception sociale de la féminité', *Actes de la Recherche en Sciences Sociales*, 83 (June 1990), pp. 40–51).

7   It is remarkable, for example, that one finds practically no myths justifying the sexual hierarchy (except perhaps the myth of the origin of barley [cf. P. Bourdieu, *The Logic of Practice*, p. 76] and the myth aimed at rationalizing the 'normal' position of man and woman in sexual intercourse, which I shall relate subsequently).

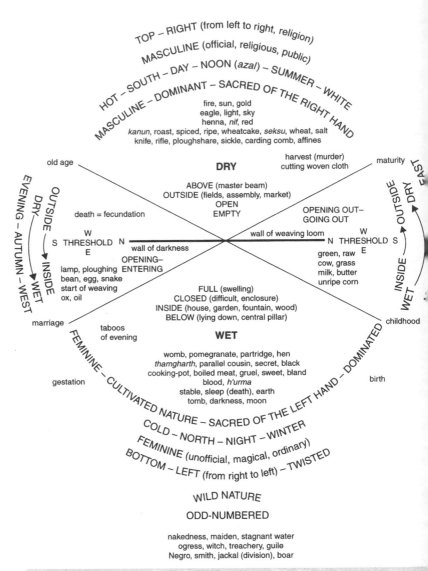

This table can be read either in terms of the vertical opposi-tions (dry/wet, top/bottom, right/left, male/female, etc.) or in terms of the processes (e.g. those of the cycle of life: marriage, gestation, birth, etc., or of the farming year) and movements (opening/closing, going in/coming out, etc.).

Synoptic diagram of pertinent oppositions

women, or, within the house, between the male part, the hearth, and the female part – the stable, the water and vegetable stores; it is the structure of time, the day and the farming year, or the cycle of life, with its male moments of rupture and the long female periods of gestation.[8]

The social world constructs the body as a sexually defined reality and as the depository of sexually defining principles of vision and division. This embodied social programme of perception is applied to all the things of the world and firstly to the *body* itself, in its biological reality. It is this programme which constructs the difference between the biological sexes in conformity with the principles of a mythic vision of the world rooted in the arbitrary relationship of domination of men over women, itself inscribed, with the division of labour, in the reality of the social order. The *biological* difference between the *sexes*, i.e. between the male and female bodies, and, in particular, the *anatomical* difference between the sex organs, can thus appear as the natural justification of the socially constructed difference between the *genders*, and in particular of the social division of labour. (The body and its movements, matrices of universals that are subject to work of social construction, are neither completely determined in their significance, especially their sexual significance, nor completely undetermined, so that the symbolism that is attached to them is both conventional and 'motivated', and therefore perceived as quasi-natural.) Because the social principle of vision constructs the anatomical difference and because this socially constructed difference becomes the basis and apparently natural justification of the social vision which founds it, there is thus a relationship of circular causality which confines thought within the self-evidence of relations of domination inscribed both in objectivity, in the form of objective divisions, and in subjectivity, in the form of cognitive

---

8 Here one would need to be able to reprise the whole analysis of the mythico-ritual system (for example, on the structure of the internal space of the house, cf. P. Bourdieu, *The Logic of Practice*, pp. 271–83; the organization of the day, pp. 253–9; and the organization of the farming year, pp. 219–48). Since here I can only mention the minimum strictly necessary for the construction of the model, I must invite readers who wish to give the ethnographic 'analyser' its full strength to consult *The Logic of Practice*, or, at least, the synoptic table reproduced here.

schemes which, being organized in accordance with these divisions, organize the perception of these objective divisions.

Manliness, virility, in its ethical aspect, i.e. as the essence of the *vir*, *virtus*, the point of honour (*nif*), the principle of the conservation and increase of honour, remains indissociable, tacitly at least, from physical virility, in particular through the attestations of sexual potency – deflowering of the bride, abundant male offspring, etc. – which are expected of a 'real' man. Hence the phallus, always metaphorically present but very rarely named, concentrates all the collective fantasies of fecundating potency.[9] Like the doughnuts or the wheat-cake, eaten on the occasion of births, circumcisions and the cutting of teeth, it 'rises' or 'raises'. The ambiguous scheme of *swelling* is the generative principle of the rites of fertility which aim to induce swelling mimetically (the phallus and the womb), in particular through recourse to 'swelling' foods and which are called for at the times when the fecundating action of male potency must be exercised, such as marriages – and also at the start of ploughing, the occasion of a homologous action of opening and insemination of the earth.[10]

The structural ambiguity, manifested by the existence of a morphological link (for example, between *abbuch*, the penis, and its feminine form, *thabbucht*, the breast), of a number of symbols linked to fertility can be explained by the fact that they represent different manifestations of the fullness of life, of the living thing that gives life (through milk and semen assimilated to milk:[11] when a man is away for a long time, his wife is told he will bring her back 'a pitcher of whey, curdled milk'; a man who is indiscreet in his extramarital relations is said to have 'spilt whey on his beard'; *yecca yeswa*, 'he has

---

9 The European tradition associates physical or moral courage with virility ('to have balls . . .') and, like the Berber tradition, explicitly makes a link between the size of the nose (*nif*), the symbol of the 'point of honour', and the supposed size of the phallus.

10 On foods that swell, like *ufthyen*, cf. P. Bourdieu, *The Logic of Practice*, pp. 250–3, and on the function of mythically ambiguous, overdetermined or 'fuzzy' acts or objects, pp. 262ff.

11 The most evocative term is *ambul*, literally meaning bladder, sausage, but also phallus (cf. T. Yacine-Titouh, 'Anthropologie de la peur. L'exemple des rapports hommes-femmes, Algérie', in T. Yacine-Titouh (ed.), *Amour, phantasmes et société en Afrique du Nord et au Sahara* (Paris: L'Harmattan, 1992), pp. 3–27; and 'La féminité et la représentation de la peur', *Cahiers de Littérature Orale*, INALCO, no. 34 (1993), pp. 19–43).

eaten and drunk', means that he has made love; to resist seduction is 'not to spill whey on one's chest'). The same morphological relation is found between *thamellalts*, the egg, the symbol par excellence of female fertility, and *imellalen*, the testicles; it is said that the penis is the only male that sits on two eggs. And the same associations are found in the words designating semen, *zzel* and especially *laâmara*, which through its root *aâmmar*, to fill, prosper, etc., evokes plenitude, that which is full of life and fills with life: the scheme of *filling* (full/empty, fertile/sterile, etc.) is regularly combined with the scheme of swelling in the generation of fertility rites.[12]

By associating phallic erection with the vital dynamic of swelling which is immanent in the whole process of natural reproduction (germination, gestation, etc.), the social *construction* of the sexual organs *records* and symbolically *ratifies* certain indisputable natural properties. Together with other mechanisms, the most important of which is undoubtedly, as has been seen, the insertion of each relationship (full/empty, for example) into a system of homologous and interconnected relationships, it thereby helps to transmute the arbitrary of the social *nomos* into a necessity of nature (*phusis*). (This logic of the *symbolic consecration* of objective processes, in particular cosmic and biological ones, which is at work in the whole mythico-ritual system – with, for example, the germination of grain treated as a resurrection, an event homologous with the rebirth of the grandfather in the grandson, sanctioned by the return of the forename – gives a quasi-objective basis to this system and hence to the belief, also reinforced by its unanimity, of which it is the object.)

When the dominated apply to what dominates them schemes that are the product of domination, or, to put it another way, when their thoughts and perceptions are structured in accordance with the very structures of the relation of domination that is imposed on them, their acts of *cognition* are, inevitably, acts of *recognition*, submission. But however close the correspondence between the realities of processes of the natural world and the principles of vision and division that are applied to them, there is always room for a *cognitive struggle* over the meaning of the things of the world and in particular of sexual

12 On the scheme full/empty and on filling, cf. P. Bourdieu, *The Logic of Practice*, pp. 277–8, and also pp. 241–2 (on the snake).

realities. The partial indeterminacy of certain objects authorizes antagonistic interpretations, offering the dominated a possibility of resistance to the effect of symbolic imposition. Thus women can draw on the dominant schemes of perception (top/bottom, hard/soft, straight/curved, dry/wet, etc.), which lead them to form a very negative view of their own genitals,[13] in order to understand the male sexual attributes by analogy with things that hang limply, without vigour (*laâlaleq, asaâlaq*, also used for onions or meat threaded on a string, or *acherbub*, the limp, lifeless penis of an old man, sometimes associated with *ajerbub*, rag);[14] and they can even draw advantage from the diminished state of the male member to assert the superiority of the female sexual organ, as in the saying: 'You, all your tackle (*laâlaleq*) dangles, says the woman to the man, whereas I am a welded stone.'[15]

Thus the social definition of the sex organs, far from being a simple recording of natural properties, directly offered to perception, is the product of a construction implying a series of oriented choices, or, more precisely, based on an accentuation of certain differences and the scotomization of certain similarities. The representation of the vagina as an inverted phallus, which Marie-Christine Pouchelle has discovered in the writings of a surgeon of the Middle Ages, obeys the same fundamental oppositions between positive and negative, up and down, that come into play as soon as the masculine principle is posited as the measure of all things.[16] Knowing thus that man and woman

13   Women consider that their genitals are beautiful only when hidden ('the welded stone' (*yejmaâ*) or placed under the protection of *serr*, the charm (unlike the male organ, which has no *serr*, because it cannot be hidden). One of the words designating the vagina, *takhna*, is, like the French *con*, used as an expletive (*A takhna!*) to express stupidity (a '*takhna* face' is a flat, amorphous face, without the relief given by a fine *nose*). Another of the Berber words designating the vagina, and one of the most pejorative, *achermid*, also means sticky.
14   All these words are of course taboo, as are some apparently anodyne terms such as *duzan*, things, tools, *laqlul*, crockery, *lah'wal*, ingredients, or *azaâkuk*, tail, which often serve as euphemistic alternatives. Among the Kabyles, as in our own tradition, the male sex organs are, euphemistically at least, referred to as *tools, instruments* – which is perhaps related to the fact that, even today, the manipulation of technical objects is systematically assigned to men.
15   Cf. Yacine-Titouh, 'Anthropologie de la peur'.
16   M.-C. Pouchelle, *Corps et chirurgie à l'apogée du Moyen Age* (Paris: Flammarion, 1983).

are perceived as two variants, superior and inferior, of the same physiology, one understands why it is that, until the Renaissance, there were no anatomical terms to describe in detail the female genitals, which were represented as comprising the same organs as those of men, but differently organized;[17] and also why, as Yvonne Knibiehler shows, the early nineteenth-century anatomists (in particular, Virey), thinking in the same terms as the moralists, tried to find in the female body the justification for the social status that they assigned to it in the name of the traditional oppositions between inside and outside, sensibility and activity, passivity and reason.[18] And one would only have to follow the history of the 'discovery' of the clitoris as related by Thomas Laqueur,[19] extending it to the Freudian theory of the 'migration' of female sexuality from the clitoris to the vagina, to complete the demonstration that, far from playing the founding role that they are sometimes given, the visible differences between the male and female sex organs are a social construction which can be traced back to the principles of division of androcentric reason, itself grounded in the division of the social statuses assigned to men and women.[20]

The schemes which structure the perception of the sex organs and, even more, of sexual activity are also applied to the male or female body itself, which has its top and bottom – the boundary being marked by the *belt*, a sign of *closure* (a woman who keeps her belt *tight*, who does not *untie* it, is regarded as

17   Cf. T. W. Laqueur, 'Orgasm, generation and the politics of reproductive biology', in C. Gallagherand and T. W. Laqueur (eds), *The Making of the Modern Body: Sexuality and Society in the Nineteenth Century* (Berkeley: University of California Press, 1987).

18   Y. Knibiehler, 'Les médecins et la "nature féminine" au temps du Code civil', *Annales*, 31, no. 4 (1976), pp. 824–45.

19   T. W. Laqueur, 'Amor Veneris, vel dulcedo appeletur', in M. Feher, R. Naddaf and N. Tazi (eds), *Zone*, part III (New York: Zone, 1989).

20   Among the countless studies showing the contribution of natural history and naturalists to the *naturalization* of sexual differences (and racial differences – the logic is the same), one might cite that by Londa Schiebinger (*Nature's Body* (Boston: Beacon Press, 1993)) which shows how the naturalists 'ascribed to [the] females [of animals] the modesty they were hoping to find in their own wives and daughters'; how, after their research on the hymen, they concluded that 'only women were blessed with a hymen', the 'guardian of their chastity' and 'vestibule of the sanctuary' (pp. 93–4), and that the beard, often associated with male honour, distinguishes men from women, who are less noble (p. 120), and from other 'races'.

virtuous, chaste) and the symbolic dividing line, at least for women, between the pure and the impure.

The belt is one of the signs of the *closure* of the female body – arms crossed over the bosom, legs together, closely tied garments – which, as many analysts have shown, is still expected of women in European and American societies today.[21] It also symbolizes the sacred barrier protecting the vagina, which is socially constituted as a sacred object and therefore subjected, in accordance with Durkheim's analysis, to strict rules of avoidance or access, which very rigorously determine the conditions of consecrated contact, that is to say the legitimate – or, conversely, the profaning – agents, moments and acts. These rules, which are particularly visible in matrimonial rites, can also be observed in the United States today, in situations where a male doctor has to perform a vaginal examination. As if all the potentially sexual connotations of gynaecological examination had to be symbolically and practically neutralized, the doctor undergoes a ritual tending to maintain the barrier, symbolized by the belt, between the public person and the vagina, which are never perceived simultaneously: he first addresses a person, face to face; then, once the person to be examined has undressed, in the presence of a nurse, he examines her while she lies with a sheet covering the upper part of her body, observing a vagina that is in a sense dissociated from the person and so reduced to the status of a thing, in the presence of the nurse, to whom he addresses his remarks, speaking of the patient in the third person; finally, in a third stage, he again addresses the woman, who has dressed in his absence.[22] It is obviously because the vagina continues to be constituted as a fetish and treated as sacred, secret and taboo that trade in sex remains stigmatized both in the ordinary consciousness and in the letter of the law which denies women the choice of working as prostitutes.[23] By involving money, some male eroticism associates the search for pleasure with the brutal exercise of power over bodies reduced to the state of objects and with the sacrilege of transgressing

21   Cf. for example N. M. Henley, *Body Politics: Power, Sex and Non-verbal Communication* (Englewood Cliffs, N.J.: Prentice Hall, 1977), esp. pp. 89ff.
22   J. M. Henslin and M. A. Biggs, 'The sociology of the vaginal examination', in J. M. Henslin (ed.), *Down to Earth Sociology* (New York and Oxford: Free Press, 1991), pp. 235–47.
23   American law forbids 'living on immoral earnings', which implies that only the free gift of sex is legitimate and that the exchange of sex for money is sacrilege par excellence inasmuch as it is a trade in what is most sacred in the body (cf. G. Pheterson, 'The whore stigma, female dishonor and male unworthiness', *Social Text*, no. 37 (1993), pp. 39–64).

the law that the body (like blood) can only be given, in a purely gratuitous offering, presupposing the suspension of violence.[24]

The body has its front, the *site of sexual difference*, and its back, sexually undifferentiated and potentially female, in other words passive, submissive, as is recalled, in gesture or words, by Mediterranean insults (in particular the notorious one-finger gesture) denouncing homosexuality.[25] It has its *public* parts – face, forehead, eyes, moustache, mouth – *noble organs of self-presentation* which concentrate social identity, the point of honour, *nif*, which requires a man to face up to others and look them in the eye; and its hidden or shameful *private* parts, which honour requires a man to conceal. It is also through the mediation of the sexual division of the legitimate uses of the body that the link (asserted by psychoanalysis) between phallus and *logos* is established: the public, active uses of the upper, male part of the body – facing up, confronting (*qabel*), looking at another man in the face, in the eyes, speaking *publicly* – are the preserve of men; women, who, in Kabylia, keep away from public places, must in a sense renounce the public use of their gaze (they walk in public with eyes directed to the ground) and their speech (the only utterance that suits them is 'I don't know', the antithesis of the manly speech which is decisive, clear-cut affirmation, at the same time as being meditated and measured).[26]

Although it may appear to be the original matrix from which spring all the forms of union of two opposing principles –

24 'Money is an integral part of the representative mode of perversion. Because the perverse fantasy is in itself unintelligible and non-exchangeable, currency by its abstract character constitutes its universally intelligible equivalent' (P. Klossowksi, *Sade et Fourier* (Paris: Fata Morgana, 1974), pp. 59–60). 'With this challenge, Sade proved that the notion of value and price is contained at the very core of voluptuous emotion and that nothing is more contrary to enjoyment than the free gift' (P. Klossowski, *La Révocation de l'Édit de Nantes* (Paris: Éditions de Minuit, 1959), p. 102).
25 There is no worse insult than the words designating the man who has been 'had', 'screwed' (*maniuk, qawad*).
26 In accordance with the usual logic of the negative prejudice, the masculine representation can condemn the feminine capacities or incapacities that it demands or helps to produce. So it is said that 'the women's market is never done' – they are talkative and above all will haggle for seven days and seven nights without coming to a decision – or that, to indicate their agreement, they must say 'yes' twice.

ploughshare and furrow, sky and earth, fire and water, etc. – the sexual act is itself conceived in terms of the principle of male primacy. The opposition between the sexes is set in the series of mythico-ritual oppositions – up/down, above/below, dry/moist, hot/cold (of a man who desires it is said that 'his *kanun* is red-hot', 'his pot is burning', 'his drum is heating'; women are said to have the capacity to 'douse fire', 'give coolness', 'quench thirst'), active/passive, mobile/immobile (the sexual act is compared to a millstone, with its moving upper part and its immobile lower part, fixed to the earth; or to the relation between the broom, which comes and goes, and the house).[27] It follows that the position regarded as normal is that in which the man is 'on top'. Just as the vagina no doubt owes its threatening, dangerous character to the fact that it is conceived as empty, but also as the negative *inversion of the phallus*, so the sexual position in which the woman mounts the man is explicitly condemned in a number of civilizations.[28] And the Kabyle tradition, not normally rich in justificatory discourses, appeals to a kind of myth of origin to legitimate the positions assigned to the two sexes in the division of sexual labour and, through the sexual division of the labour of production and reproduction, in the whole social order and ultimately in the cosmic order.

'It was at the fountain (*tala*) that the first man met the first woman. She was drawing water when the man arrogantly approached and asked to drink. But she had arrived first and she was thirsty too. Angrily the man jostled her. She slipped and fell to the ground. Then the man saw the woman's thighs, which were different from his own. He stood in amazement. The woman, who was more cunning, then taught him many things. "Lie down," she said, "and I will show you what your organs are for." He lay down; she caressed his penis, which became twice as large, and she lay on top of him. The man felt great pleasure. After that he followed the woman everywhere to do the same thing, for she knew more things than him, how to make fire and so on. One day the man said to the woman: "I want to show you something too; I know some things too. Lie down and I will lie on you." The woman lay on the ground and the man lay on top of her. He felt

27   Cf. Yacine-Titouh, 'Anthropologie de la peur'.
28   According to Charles Malamoud, in Sanskrit it is referred to as *Viparita*, inverted, a word that is also used to refer to the world turned upside down, topsy-turvy.

the same pleasure and then said to the woman: "At the fountain it's you [who dominate]; in the house, it's me." In the mind of man, it is always the last words that count, and since then men have always liked to be on top of women. That is how they became the masters and why they must be in charge.'[29]

The intention of sociodicy is here unequivocal: at the very origin of culture understood as a social order dominated by the male principle, the founding myth institutes the constituting opposition (in fact, already in play, through for example the opposition between the fountain and the house, in the assumptions made to justify it) between nature and culture, between the 'sexuality' of nature and the 'sexuality' of culture. In opposition to the anomic act performed beside the fountain, the female place par excellence, and initiated by the woman, the perverse seductress, naturally informed of matters of love, stands the act subject to *nomos*, domestic and domesticated, performed at the behest of the man and conforming to the order of things, the fundamental hierarchy of the social order and the cosmic order, and in the house, the site of cultivated nature, the legitimate domination of the male principle over the female principle, symbolized by the pre-eminence of the master beam (*asalas alemmas*) over the vertical pillar (*thigejdith*), a female fork open to the sky.

On top or underneath, active or passive – these parallel alternatives describe the sexual act as a relation of domination. To possess sexually, as in the French *baiser* or the English 'to fuck', is to dominate in the sense of subjecting to one's power, but also to deceive, mislead, or, as we say, 'to have' (whereas to resist seduction is not to be deceived, not 'to be had'). The manifestations of virility, whether legitimate or illegitimate, belong to the logic of prowess, the exploit, which confers honour. And although the extreme gravity of the slightest sexual transgression forbids open expression of this, the indirect challenge to the masculinity of other men that is implied in every assertion of virility contains the principle of the agonistic vision of male sexuality which is declared more overtly in other parts of the Mediterranean area and beyond.

29   Cf. Yacine-Titouh, 'Anthropologie de la peur'.

A political sociology of the sexual act would show that, as is always the case in a relation of domination, the practices and representations of the two sexes are in no way symmetrical. Not only because, even in contemporary European and American societies, young men and women have very different points of view on the love relation, which men most often conceive in terms of conquest (especially in conversations between friends, which give a prominent place to boasting about female conquests),[30] but also because the sexual act itself is seen by men as a form of domination, appropriation, 'possession'. Hence the discrepancy between the probable expectations of men and women as regards sexuality – and the misunderstandings, linked to misinterpretation of sometimes deliberately ambiguous or deceptive 'signals', which result from this. In contrast to women, who are socially prepared to see sexuality as an intimate and emotionally highly charged experience which does not necessarily include penetration but which can contain a wide range of activities (talking, touching, caressing, embracing, etc.),[31] men are inclined to compartmentalize sexuality, which is conceived as an aggressive and essentially physical act of conquest oriented towards penetration and orgasm.[32] And although, on this point like all the others, there are of course very great variations according to social position,[33] age – and previous experience – it can be inferred from a series of interviews that apparently symmetrical practices (such as fellatio and cunnilingus) tend to have very different significance for men (who are inclined to see them as acts of domination, through the submission and pleasure obtained) and for women. Male pleasure is, in part, enjoyment of female pleasure, of the power to give pleasure; and so Catherine MacKinnon is no doubt right to see the faking of orgasm as a perfect example of the male power to make the interaction between the sexes conform to the view of it held by men, who expect the female orgasm

30   Cf. B. Ehrenreich, *The Hearts of Men: American Dreams and the Flight from Commitment* (Garden City, N.Y.: Doubleday Anchor, 1983); E. Anderson, *Streetwise: Race, Class and Change in an Urban Community* (Chicago: Chicago University Press, 1990).

31   D. Baca-Zinn and S. Eitzen, *Diversity in American Families* (New York: Harper and Row, 1990), pp. 249–54; L. Rubin, *Intimate Strangers* (New York: Basic Books, 1983).

32   D. Russell, *The Politics of Rape* (New York: Stein and Day, 1975), p. 272; D. Russell, *Sexual Exploitation* (Beverly Hills: Sage, 1984), p. 162.

33   Although for the sake of argument I have been led to speak of men and women without reference to their social position, I am aware that one would need to take account in each case, and, as I shall several times in the subsequent text, of the specifications that the principle of social differentiation imposes on the principle of sexual differentiation (and vice versa).

to provide a proof of their virility and the pleasure derived from this extreme form of submission.[34] Similarly, sexual harassment does not always aim at the sexual possession that seems to be its exclusive goal: in some cases it may aim at sheer possession, the pure affirmation of domination in its pure state.[35]

If the sexual relation appears as a social relation of domination, this is because it is constructed through the fundamental principle of division between the active male and the passive female and because this principle creates, organizes, expresses and directs desire – male desire as the desire for possession, eroticized domination, and female desire as the desire for masculine domination, as eroticized subordination or even, in the limiting case, as the eroticized recognition of domination. In a case where, as in homosexual relations, reciprocity is possible, the links between sexuality and power are revealed with particular clarity and the roles taken in sexual relations, especially active and passive ones, appear as indissociable from the relations between the social positions which determine both their possibility and their meaning. Penetration, especially when performed on a man, is one of the affirmations of the *libido dominandi* that is never entirely absent from the masculine libido. It is known that in a number of societies homosexual possession is conceived as a manifestation of 'power', an act of domination (performed as such, in some cases, in order to assert superiority by 'feminizing' the other) and that, understood in this way, among the Greeks, it condemned the victim to dishonour and the loss of the status of a complete man and a citizen,[36] while for a Roman citizen, 'passive' homosexuality with a slave was regarded as monstrous.[37] Likewise, according to John Boswell, 'penetration and power were associated with the prerogatives of the ruling male elite; surrendering to penetration was a symbolic abrogation of power and

---

34   C. A. MacKinnon, *Feminism Unmodified: Discourses on Life and Law* (Cambridge, Mass.: Harvard University Press, 1987), p. 58.
35   Cf. R. Christin, 'Possession', in P. Bourdieu et al., *The Weight of the World* (Cambridge: Polity, 2000), pp. 309–16.
36   Cf. for example K. J. Dover, *Greek Homosexuality* (Cambridge, Mass.: Harvard University Press, 1989).
37   P. Veyne, 'L'Homosexualité à Rome', *Communications*, 35 (1982), pp. 26–32.

authority.'[38] It can be understood that from this point of view, which links sexuality and power, the worst humiliation for a man is to be turned into a woman; and one might evoke here the testimonies of men who, as a result of torture deliberately designed to *feminize* them, particularly through sexual humiliation, jokes about their virility, accusations of homosexuality, etc., or simply the need to behave as if they were women, have come to discover 'what it means to be constantly aware of one's body, always exposed to humiliation or ridicule, and to find comfort in household tasks or chatting with friends'.[39]

The embodiment of domination

Whereas the idea that the social definition of the body, and especially of the sexual organs, is the product of a social labour of construction has become quite banal through having been advocated by the whole anthropological tradition, the mechanism of the inversion of cause and effect that I am trying to describe here, through which the naturalization of that construction takes place, has not, it seems to me, been fully described. For the paradox is that it is the visible differences between the female body and the male body which, being perceived and constructed according to the practical schemes of the androcentric worldview, become the most perfectly indisputable guarantee of meanings and values that are in harmony with the principles of that worldview: it is not the phallus (or its absence) which is the basis of that worldview, rather it is that worldview which, being organized according to the division into *relational genders*, male and female, can institute the phallus, constituted as the symbol of virility, of the specifically male point of honour (*nif*), and the difference between biologi-

38   J. Boswell, 'Sexual and ethical categories in premodern Europe', in P. McWhirter, S. Sanders and J. Reinisch (eds), *Homosexuality/Heterosexuality: Concepts of Sexual Orientation* (New York: Oxford University Press, 1990), p. 17.
39   Cf. J. Franco, 'Gender, death and resistance: facing the ethical vacuum', in J. E. Corradi, P. Weiss Fagen and M. A. Garretón (eds), *Fear at the Edge: State Terror and Resistance in Latin America* (Berkeley: University of California Press, 1992).

cal bodies as objective foundations of the difference between the sexes, in the sense of genders constructed as two hierarchized social essences. Far from the necessities of biological reproduction determining the symbolic organization of the sexual division of labour and, ultimately, of the whole natural and social order, it is an arbitrary construction of the male and female body, of its uses and functions, especially in biological reproduction, which gives an apparently natural foundation to the androcentric view of the division of sexual labour and the sexual division of labour and so of the whole cosmos. The particular strength of the masculine sociodicy comes from the fact that it combines and condenses two operations: it legitimates a relationship of domination by embedding it in a biological nature that is itself a naturalized social construction.

The work of symbolic construction is far more than a strictly *performative* operation of naming which orients and structures *representations*, starting with representations of the body (which is itself not negligible); it is brought about and culminates in a profound and durable transformation of bodies (and minds), that is to say, in and through a process of practical construction imposing a *differentiated definition* of the legitimate uses of the body, in particular sexual ones, which tends to exclude from the universe of the feasible and thinkable everything that marks membership of the other gender – and in particular all the potentialities biologically implied in the 'polymorphous perversity', as Freud puts it, of every infant – to produce the social artefact of the manly man or the womanly woman. The arbitrary *nomos* which institutes the two classes in objectivity takes on the appearance of a law of nature (people often speak of a sexuality or, even today, a marriage that is 'against nature') only at the end of a *somatization of the social relations of domination*: it is only after a formidable collective labour of diffuse and continuous socialization that the distinctive identities instituted by the cultural arbitrary are embodied in habitus that are clearly differentiated according to the dominant principle of division and capable of perceiving the world according to this principle.

Existing only *relationally*, each of the two genders is the product of the labour of diacritical construction, both theoretical and practical, which is necessary in order to produce it as a body *socially differentiated* from the opposite gender (in all the culturally pertinent respects), i.e. as a male, and therefore non-female, habitus or as a female and therefore non-male habitus. The formative process, *Bildung*, in the full sense, which brings about this social construction of the body only very partially takes the form of explicit and express pedagogic action. It is to a large extent the automatic, agentless effect of a physical and social order entirely organized in accordance with the andro-centric principle (which explains the extreme strength of its hold). Inscribed in the things of the world, the masculine order also inscribes itself in bodies through the tacit injunctions that are implied in the routines of the division of labour or of collective or private rituals (consider, for example, the avoidance behaviours imposed on women by their exclusion from male spaces). The regularities of the physical order and the social order impose and inculcate dispositions by excluding women from the noblest tasks (leading the plough, for example), by designating inferior places for them (the edge of the road or embankment, for example), by teaching them how to hold their bodies (for example, bent, with arms folded on the chest, before respectable men), by assigning them menial and drudging tasks (they transport dung, and when olives are harvested, they and the children pick them up from the ground while the men wield the pole to knock them down), and, more generally, by taking advantage, in accordance with the fundamental presup-positions, of biological differences, which thus appear to be at the basis of social differences.

In the long sequence of silent calls to order, rites of institu-tion occupy a place apart, by virtue of their solemn and extra-ordinary character: they aim to set up, in the name of the whole assembled community, a sacralizing separation not only, as is suggested by the notion of the rite of passage, between those who have *already* received the *distinctive mark* and those who have *not yet* received it, because they are too young, but also and more importantly between those who are socially worthy to receive it and those who are *forever excluded* from it, in other words the women;[40] or, as in the case of circumcision, the rite

40　To the contribution which rites of institution make to the instituting of manliness in male bodies should be added all children's games, especially

of institution of masculinity par excellence, between those whose manliness it consecrates and those who cannot undergo the initiation and who cannot fail to see themselves as lacking what constitutes the occasion and the matter of the ritual of confirmation of manliness.

Thus, what the mythic discourse professes in an ultimately rather naive way is enacted by rites of institution in a more insidious and symbolically no doubt more effective way; and these rites take their places in the series of operations of *differentiation* aimed at accentuating in each man or woman the external signs most immediately corresponding to the social definition of his or her sexual *distinction* or encouraging the practices appropriate to his or her sex while forbidding or discouraging inappropriate behaviours, especially in relations with the opposite sex. This is the case, for example, of the so-called rites of 'separation', which aim to emancipate the boy from his mother and to ensure his gradual masculinization by encouraging and preparing him to confront the external world. Anthropological inquiry reveals that the psychological work which, according to one psychoanalytical tradition,[41] boys must perform in order to break free of their quasi-symbiosis with their mother and to assert their own sexuality is expressly and explicitly accompanied and even organized by the group, which, in the whole series of sexual rites of institution oriented towards virilization and, more generally, in all the differentiated and differentiating practices of ordinary existence (manly sports and games, hunting, etc.), encourages

those which have a more or less obvious sexual connotation (such as the contest to urinate as far as possible, or the homosexual games of shepherd boys) and which, in their apparent insignificance, are highly charged with ethical connotations, often inscribed in language (for example, in Béarnais, *picheprim*, 'short-piss', means ungenerous, miserly). On the reasons which led me to substitute the notion of rite of institution (a term that should be understood in the sense both of what is instituted – the institution of marriage – and the act of instituting – the instituting of the heir) for the notion of rite of passage, which probably owed its immediate success to the fact that it is simply a prenotion of common sense converted into a scientific-looking concept; see P. Bourdieu, 'Les rites d'institution' (in *Ce que parler veut dire* (Paris: Fayard, 1982), pp. 121–34).
41   Cf. in particular N. J. Chodorow, *The Reproduction of Mothering: Psychoanalysis and the Sociology of Gender* (Berkeley: University of California Press, 1978).

the break with the maternal world, from which girls (and also, to their misfortune, the 'sons of the widow') are exempted – which enables them to live in a kind of continuity with their mothers.[42]

The objective 'intention' of denying the female part of the male (the very one which Melanie Klein asked psychoanalysis to recover, through an opposite operation to that performed by ritual), of severing attachments to the mother, the earth, the moist, night, nature, is manifested for example in the rites performed at the moment called 'the separation in *ennayer*' (*el âazla gennayer*), such as boys' first haircut, and in all the ceremonies which mark the crossing of the *threshold* of the male world and which culminate in circumcision. Countless acts aim to separate the boy from his mother – using objects made with fire and tending to symbolize *cutting* (and male sexuality): knife, dagger, ploughshare, etc. For example, a newborn boy is placed on the right-hand (male) side of his mother, who herself lies on her right side, and between them are placed typically male objects such as a carding comb, a large knife, a ploughshare, one of the hearth-stones. Likewise, the importance of the first haircut is linked to the fact that the hair, female in nature, is one of the symbolic links that bind the boy to the maternal world. It falls to the father to perform this inaugural cut, with a razor, a male implement, on the day of the 'separation in *ennayer*', shortly before the boy's first visit to the market, i.e. at an age between six and ten. And the entry into the market – the boy's introduction to the world of men, the point of honour and symbolic struggles – continues the work of virilization (or defeminization): dressed in new clothes and wearing a silk belt in his hair, he is given a dagger, a padlock and a mirror, while his mother places a fresh egg in the cape of his burnous. At the gate of the market he breaks the egg and opens the padlock – manly acts of defloration – and looks at himself in the mirror, which, like the threshold, is an operator of reversal. His father guides him into the market, an exclusively male world, and introduces him to the other men. On the way back, they buy an ox's head, a phallic symbol – on account of its horns – associated with *nif*.

42   As opposed to those who are sometimes called in Kabylia 'the sons of men', whose upbringing falls to several men, the 'sons of the widow' are suspected of having missed out on the unremitting labour that is needed to prevent boys from becoming women and of having been abandoned to the feminizing action of their mothers.

The same psychosomatic work which, when applied to boys, aims to virilize them by stripping them of everything female which may remain in them – as it does in the 'sons of the widow' – takes a more radical form when applied to girls. Because woman is constituted as a negative entity, defined only by default, even her virtues can only be affirmed by a double negation, as vice denied or overcome, or as lesser evils. All the work of socialization therefore tends to impose limits on her, which all concern the body, thus defined as sacred, h'aram, and which have to be inscribed in the dispositions of the body. So the young Kabyle woman internalized the fundamental principles of the female 'art of living', of proper demeanour and deportment, inseparably corporeal and moral, by learning how to put on and wear the different clothing corresponding to her successive stages of life – little girl, nubile maiden, wife, mother – and insensibly acquiring, as much by unconscious mimicry as by express obedience, the right way to tie her belt or her hair, to move or keep still this or that part of her body when walking, to present her face and turn her eyes.

This apprenticeship is all the more effective because it remains essentially tacit: femininity is imposed for the most part through an unremitting discipline that concerns every part of the body and is continuously recalled through the constraints of clothing or hairstyle. The antagonistic principles of male and female identity are thus laid down in the form of permanent stances, gaits and postures which are the realization, or rather, the naturalization of an ethic. Just as the ethic of male honour can be summed up in a word, endlessly repeated by informants, qabel, to face, face up to, and in the upright posture (our military 'attention'), the visible sign of rectitude, which it designates,[43] so female submissiveness seems to find a natural translation in bending, stooping, lowering oneself, 'submitting' – curved and supple postures and the associated docility being seen as appropriate to women. Early upbringing tends to inculcate ways of bearing the body, or various parts of it, the male right hand and the female left hand, ways of walking,

43 On the word qabel, itself linked to the most fundamental orientations of space and of the whole worldview, cf. P. Bourdieu, *The Logic of Practice*, p. 90.

holding the head or directing the gaze, directly in the eyes or at one's feet, etc., which are charged with an ethic, a politics and a cosmology. (Our whole ethics, not to mention our aesthetics, is contained in the system of cardinal adjectives high/low, straight/twisted, rigid/supple, open/closed, etc., a good proportion of which also designate positions or dispositions of the body or some part of it, e.g. 'head held high', 'eyes downcast'.)

The submissive demeanour which is imposed on Kabyle women is the limiting case of what is still imposed on women, even today, as much in the United States as in Europe, and which, as a number of observers have shown, is summed up in a few imperatives: smile, look down, accept interruptions, etc. Nancy M. Henley has shown how women are taught to occupy space, to walk, to adopt appropriate postures. Using a method called 'memory work', which aims to evoke stories of childhood, discussed and interpreted collectively, Frigga Haug has also tried to bring to light the feelings linked to various parts of the body – the back which has to be kept straight, the stomach which has to be held in, the legs which must be kept together, etc., all postures which are charged with moral significance (it is vulgar to sit with the legs apart, a large stomach indicates lack of willpower, etc.).[44] As if femininity were measured by the art of 'shrinking' (in Berber the feminine is marked by the diminutive form), women are held in a kind of *invisible enclosure* (of which the veil is only the visible manifestation) circumscribing the space allowed for the movements and postures of their bodies (whereas men occupy more space, especially in public places). This symbolic *confinement* is secured practically by their clothing which (as was even more visible in former times) has the effect not only of masking the body but of continuously calling it to order (the skirt fulfils a function entirely analogous to that of the priest's cassock) without ever needing to prescribe or proscribe anything explicitly ('my mother never told me not to sit with my legs apart') – either because it constrains movement in

44 F. Haug et al., *Female Sexualization: A Collective Work of Memory* (London: Verso, 1987). Although the authors do not seem to be aware of it, this inculcation of the submission of the body, which encounters the complicity of women, despite the constraint it imposes on them, is strongly marked socially, and the embodiment of femininity is inseparable from an *embodiment of distinction*, or, to put it another way, from contempt for the vulgarity associated with plunging necklines, too-short mini-skirts and too-heavy make-up (although this is generally perceived as very 'feminine' . . .).

various ways, like high heels or the bag which constantly encumbers the hands, and above all the skirt which prevents or hinders certain activities (running, various ways of sitting, etc.), or because it allows them only at the cost of constant precautions, as with young women who constantly pull at a too-short skirt, use their forearms to cover a plunging neckline or have to perform acrobatics to pick up an object while keeping their legs together.[45] These ways of bearing the body, which are very deeply associated with the moral restraint and the demureness that are appropriate for women, continue to impose themselves unconsciously on women even when they cease to be imposed by clothing (like the small, quick steps of some young women wearing trousers and flat heels). And the relaxed poses and postures, such as leaning back on two legs of a chair or putting the feet on a desk, which some men – especially those of high status – sometimes allow themselves as a sign of power or, which amounts to the same thing, of self-assurance, are literally unthinkable for women.[46]

To those who may object that many women have now broken with the traditional norms and forms of restraint and who see the scope now available for the controlled exhibition of the body as an index of 'liberation', it only has to be pointed out that this use of the body remains very obviously subordinated to the male point of view (as is clearly seen in the use made of women's bodies in advertising, even today, in France, after half a century of feminism). The female body at once offered and refused manifests the symbolic availability which, as a number of feminist works have shown, is incumbent upon women, the combination of a power of attraction and seduction that is known and recognized by all, both men and women, and tending to honour the men on whom they depend or to

45   Cf. Henley, *Body Politics*, pp. 38, 89–91, and also pp. 142–4, the reproduction of a cartoon with the caption 'Exercises for men', showing the 'absurdity of the postures' expected of women.
46   Everything that remains in the implicit state in the ordinary learning of femininity is made explicit in finishing schools with their courses in deportment and entertaining, in which, as Yvette Delsaut has observed, girls learn how to walk and stand (hands behind the back, feet side by side), how to smile, how to go up and down stairs (without looking at the feet), how to behave at table ('the hostess must ensure that everything happens smoothly, without anyone noticing'), how to speak to guests ('charm and politeness'), how to dress ('no garish, aggressive colours') and how to use make-up.

whom they are linked, and a duty of selective refusal which adds the price of exclusivity to the effect of 'conspicuous consumption'.

The divisions constitutive of the social order and, more precisely, the social relations of domination and exploitation that are instituted between the sexes thus progressively embed themselves in two different classes of habitus, in the form of opposed and complementary bodily *hexis* and principles of vision and division which lead to the classifying of all the things of the world and all practices according to distinctions that are reducible to the male/female opposition. It falls to men, who belong on the side of all things external, official, public, straight, high and discontinuous, to perform all the brief, dangerous and spectacular acts which, like the sacrifice of the ox, ploughing or harvesting, not to mention murder or war, mark breaks in the ordinary course of life; women, by contrast, being on the side of things that are internal, damp, low, curved and continuous, are assigned all domestic labour, in other words the tasks that are private and hidden, even invisible or shameful, such as the care of the children or the animals, as well as all the external tasks that are attributed to them by mythic reason, that is to say, those that involve water, grass and other green vegetation (such as hoeing and gardening), milk and wood, and especially the dirtiest, most monotonous and menial tasks. Because the whole of the finite world in which they are confined – the space of the village, the house, language, tools – contains the same silent calls to order, women can only *become what they are* according to mythic reason, thus confirming, and first in their own eyes, that they are naturally consigned to what is low, twisted, picayune, futile, menial, etc. They are condemned to give at every moment the appearances of a natural foundation to the diminished identity that is socially bestowed on them: they are the ones who perform the long, thankless, tedious task of picking up from the ground the olives or twigs that the men have brought down with a pole or an axe; they are the ones who, delegated to the vulgar preoccupations of the everyday management of the domestic economy, seem to take pleasure in the petty calculations of debt and interest to which the man of honour does not stoop. (Thus I have a childhood memory from Béarn of the men, neighbours and friends, who had killed the pig in the morning, after a brief and somewhat ostentatious display of violence – the screech of the escaping animal, the wielding of big knives, the gush of blood, etc. – sitting all afternoon, and sometimes until the next morning, playing cards, barely pausing to lift a too-heavy cauldron, while the women of the house would bustle about preparing sausages, puddings and pâtés.) The men (and the women themselves) remain unaware that it is the logic of the relationship of domination which imposes on and inculcates in women not only the virtues that morality requires of them but also all the negative properties that the dominant view imputes to their *nature*, like cunning or, to take a more favourable feature, intuition.

What is called 'female intuition', a particular form of the special lucidity of the dominated, is, even in our own world, inseparable from the objective and subjective submissiveness which encourages or constrains the attentiveness and vigilance needed to anticipate desires or avoid unpleasantness. A good deal of research has brought to light the special perspicacity of the dominated, particularly women (and more especially of women who are doubly or triply dominated, like the black housemaids described by Judith Rollins in *Between Women*).[47] Women are more sensitive than men to non-verbal cues (especially tone) and are better at identifying an emotion represented non-verbally and decoding the implicit content of a dialogue;[48] according to a survey by two Dutch researchers, they are capable of describing their husbands in great detail, whereas men can only describe their wives in very broad stereotypes valid for 'women in general'.[49] The same authors suggest that homosexuals, who, having necessarily been raised as heterosexuals, have internalized the dominant point of view, may adopt this point of view on themselves (which condemns them to a kind of cognitive and evaluative dissonance tending to contribute to their special perspicacity) and that they understand the point of view of the dominant better than the dominant understand theirs.

47 J. Rollins, *Between Women: Domestics and their Employers* (Philadelphia: Temple University Press, 1985).
48 Cf. W. N. Thompson, *Quantitative Research in Public Address and Communication* (New York: Random House, 1967), pp. 47–8.
49 Cf. A. Van Stolk and C. Wouters, 'Power changes and self-respect: a comparison of two cases of established–outsiders relations', *Theory, Culture and Society*, 4, no. 2–3 (1987), pp. 477–88.

Being symbolically condemned to resignation and discretion, women can exercise some degree of power only by turning the strength of the strong against them or by accepting the need to efface themselves and, in any case, to deny a power that they can only exercise vicariously, as '*éminences grises*'. But (as Lucien Bianco says of peasant resistance in China) 'the weapons of the weak are always weak weapons.'[50] The symbolic strategies that women use against men, such as those of magic, remain dominated, because the apparatus of symbols and mythic operators that they implement and the ends they pursue (such as the love of a loved man or the impotence of a hated man) are rooted in the androcentric view in the name of which they are dominated. These strategies, which are not strong enough really to subvert the relation of domination, at least have the effect of confirming the dominant representation of women as maleficent beings, whose purely negative identity is made up essentially of taboos each of which presents a possibility of transgression. This is true in particular of all the forms of soft violence, sometimes almost invisible, that women use against the physical or symbolic violence of men, from magic, cunning, lies or passivity (particularly in sexual relations) to the possessive love of the possessed, that of the Mediterranean mother or the mothering wife, who victimizes and induces guilt by victimizing herself and by offering her infinite devotion and mute suffering as a gift too great to be matched or as a debt that can never be repaid. Thus, whatever they do, women are condemned to furnish the proof of their malign nature and to justify the taboos and prejudice that they incur by virtue of their essential maleficence – in accordance with the logic, which can be described as tragic, whereby the social reality that produces domination often confirms the representations that domination invokes in order to justify itself.

The androcentric view is thus continuously legitimated by the very practices that it determines. Because their dispositions are the product of embodiment of the *negative prejudice* against the female that is instituted in the order of things, women cannot but constantly confirm this prejudice. The logic is that of the *curse*, in the strong sense of a pessimistic self-fulfilling

50   L. Bianco, 'Résistance paysanne', *Actuel Marx*, no. 22 (1997), pp. 138–52.

prophecy calling for its own validation and bringing about what it foretells. It is at work, daily, in a number of exchanges between the sexes: the same dispositions that incline men to leave women to deal with menial tasks and thankless, petty procedures (such as, in our societies, finding out prices, checking bills, asking for discounts), in short, to disencumber themselves of all the behaviours incompatible with their dignity, also lead them to accuse women of 'petty-mindedness' and 'mean-spiritedness' and even to blame them if they fail in the undertakings that have been abandoned to them, without giving them any credit if things go well.[51]

Symbolic violence

All the conditions for the full exercise of male domination are thus combined. The precedence universally accorded to men is affirmed in the objectivity of the social structures and the productive or reproductive activities, based on a sexual division of the labour of biological and social production and reproduction which gives the better part to men, and also in the schemes immanent in everyone's habitus. These schemes, shaped by similar conditions, and therefore objectively harmonized, function as matrices of the perceptions, thoughts and actions of all members of the society – historical transcendentals which, being shared by all, impose themselves on each agent as transcendent. As a consequence, the androcentric representation of biological reproduction and social reproduction is invested with the objectivity of a common sense, a practical, doxic consensus on the sense of practices. And women themselves apprehend all reality, and in particular the power relations in which they

51 The interviews and observations that we made in the course of our research into the economy of the production of real estate gave us many opportunities to verify that this logic is still at work, even today and close to us (cf. P. Bourdieu, 'Un contrat sous contrainte', *Actes de la Recherche en Sciences Sociales*, 81–2 (Mar. 1990), pp. 34–51). Although men can no longer always affect the same haughty disdain for the petty preoccupations of the economy (except perhaps in the cultural universes), it is not uncommon for them to assert their statutory loftiness, especially when in positions of authority, by manifesting their indifference to subordinate questions of practicality, which are often left to women.

are held, through schemes of thought that are the product of embodiment of those power relations and which are expressed in the founding oppositions of the symbolic order. It follows that their acts of cognition are acts of practical recognition, doxic acceptance, a belief that does not need to be thought and affirmed as such, and which in a sense 'makes' the symbolic violence which it undergoes.[52]

Although I have no illusions as to my ability to dispel all misunderstanding in advance, I would simply like to warn against the radical misinterpretations often made of the notion of symbolic violence, which all arise from a more or less reductive understanding of the adjective 'symbolic', which is used here in a sense that I believe to be rigorous, and whose theoretical basis I set out in an article two decades ago.[53] Taking 'symbolic' in one of its commonest senses, people sometimes assume that to emphasize symbolic violence is to minimize the role of physical violence, to forget (and make people forget) that there are battered, raped and exploited women, or worse, to seek to exculpate men from that form of violence – which is obviously not the case. Understanding 'symbolic' as the opposite of 'real, actual', people suppose that symbolic violence is a purely 'spiritual' violence which ultimately has no real effects. It is this naive distinction, characteristic of a crude materialism, that the materialist theory of the economy of symbolic goods, which I have been trying to build up over many years, seeks to destroy, by giving its proper place in theory to the objectivity of the subjective experience of relations of domination. Another misunderstanding: the reference to ethnology, of which I have tried to show the heuristic functions here, is suspected of being a way of restoring the myth of the 'eternal feminine' (or masculine) or, worse, of eternalizing the structure of masculine domination by describing it as unvarying and eternal. On the contrary, far from asserting that the structures of domination are ahistorical, I shall try to establish that they are *the product of an incessant (and therefore historical) labour of reproduction*, to which singular agents (including men, with weapons such as physical violence and symbolic violence) and institutions – families, the church, the educational system, the state – contribute.

52   The verbal or non-verbal cues which designate the symbolically dominant position (that of man, noble, chief, etc.) can only be understood by people who have learned the 'code' (rather like military 'stripes' which one has to learn how to read).
53   Cf. P. Bourdieu, 'Sur le pouvoir symbolique', *Annales*, no. 3 (May–June 1977), pp. 405–11.

The dominated apply categories constructed from the point of view of the dominant to the relations of domination, thus making them appear as natural. This can lead to a kind of systematic self-depreciation, even self-denigration, visible in particular, as has been seen, in the representation that Kabyle women have of their genitals as something deficient, ugly, even repulsive (or, in modern societies, in the vision that many women have of their bodies as not conforming to the aesthetic canons imposed by fashion), and, more generally, in their adherence to a demeaning image of woman.[54] Symbolic violence is instituted through the adherence that the dominated cannot fail to grant to the dominant (and therefore to the domination) when, to shape her thought of him, and herself, or, rather, her thought of her relation with him, she has only cognitive instruments that she shares with him and which, being no more than the embodied form of the relation of domination, cause that relation to appear as natural; or, in other words, when the schemes she applies in order to perceive and appreciate herself, or to perceive and appreciate the dominant (high/low, male/female, white/black, etc.), are the product of the embodiment of the – thereby naturalized – classifications of which her social being is the product.

Being unable to evoke here with sufficient subtlety (it would take a Virginia Woolf to do so) sufficiently numerous, varied and cogent examples of concrete situations in which this gentle and often invisible violence is exerted, I shall simply refer to observations which, in their objectivism, are more persuasive than description of the minutiae of interactions. Surveys show, for example, that a large majority of French women say they want a husband who is older and also (quite coherently) taller than themselves; two-thirds of them even explicitly reject the idea of a husband shorter than themselves.[55] What is the

54 In interviews conducted in France in 1996, it was very common for women to say they found it difficult to accept their bodies.

55 In the same logic, Myra Marx Ferree, who points out that the main obstacle to the transformation of the division of domestic labour lies in the fact that household tasks are perceived as 'unfit for "real men"', notes that women conceal the help they receive from their husbands for fear of diminishing them (cf. M. Marx Ferree, 'Sacrifice, satisfaction and social change: employment and the family', in K. Brooklin Sacks and D. Remy (eds), *My Troubles Are Going to Have Trouble with Me* (New Brunswick, N.J.: Rutgers University Press, 1984), p. 73).

meaning of this refusal to see the disappearance of the ordinary signs of the sexual 'hierarchy'? 'Accepting an inversion of appearances', replies Michel Bozon, 'is to suggest that it is the woman who dominates, which, paradoxically, lowers her socially; she feels diminished with a diminished man.'[56] So it is not sufficient to note that women generally agree with men (who, for their part, prefer younger women) when they accept the external signs of a dominated position; in their representation of their relation with the man to which their social identity is (or will be) attached, they take account of the representation that men and women as a whole will inevitably form of him by applying to him the schemes of perception and appreciation universally shared (within the group in question). Because these common principles tacitly and unarguably demand that, at least in appearances and seen from outside, the man should occupy the dominant position within the couple, it is for him, for the sake of the dignity that they recognize *a priori* in him, but also for themselves, that they can only want and love a man whose dignity is clearly affirmed and attested in and by the fact that he is visibly 'above' them. This takes place, of course, without any calculation, through the apparent arbitrariness of an inclination that is not amenable to discussion or reason but which, as is shown by observation of the desired, and also real, differences, can only arise and be fulfilled in the experience of the superiority of which age and height (justified as indices of maturity and guarantees of security) are the most indisputable and universally recognized signs.[57]

To follow through the paradoxes that only a dispositionalist view can make intelligible, one only has to note that those who show themselves to be most submissive to the 'traditional' model – by saying

56   M. Bozon, 'Les femmes et l'écart d'âge entre conjoints: une domination consentie', I: 'Types d'union et attentes en matière d'écart d'âge', *Population*, 2 (1990), pp. 327–60; II: 'Modes d'entrée dans la vie adulte et représentations du conjoint', *Population*, 3 (1990), pp. 565–602; 'Apparence physique et choix du conjoint', *INED* [Institut National des Études Démographiques], *Congrès et colloques*, 7 (1991), pp. 91–110.
57   One might also mention here the very subtle games through which, in Kabylia, some women (of honour), although dominant in practice, were able to adopt a submissive posture enabling the man to appear and see himself as dominant.

that they wish for a larger age-gap – are found mostly among the social categories of self-employed craftsmen, shopkeepers, farmers and manual workers, in which marriage remains, for women, the prime means of acquiring a social position – as if, being the product of an unconscious adjustment to the probabilities associated with an objective structure of domination, the submissive dispositions that are expressed in these preferences produced the equivalent of what could be a calculation of enlightened self-interest. By contrast, these dispositions tend to weaken – with, no doubt, effects of *hysteresis* which would emerge from analysis of variations in practices not only according to the position occupied, but also according to trajectory – with the objective dependency that helps to produce and maintain them (the same logic of adjustment of dispositions to the objective chances also explaining why it can be observed that women's access to employment is a major factor in their access to divorce).[58] This tends to confirm that, contrary to the romantic representation of love, choice of partner is not exempt from a form of rationality that owes nothing to rational calculation, or, to put it another way, that love is often partly *amor fati*, love of one's social destiny.

So the only way to understand this particular form of domination is to move beyond the forced choice between constraint (by forces) and consent (to reasons), between mechanical coercion and voluntary, free, deliberate, even calculated submission. The effect of symbolic domination (whether ethnic, gender, cultural or linguistic, etc.) is exerted not in the pure logic of knowing consciousnesses but through the schemes of perception, appreciation and action that are constitutive of habitus and which, below the level of the decisions of consciousness and the controls of the will, set up a cognitive relationship that is profoundly obscure to itself.[59] Thus, the paradoxical logic of

58   Cf. B. Bastard and L. Cardia-Vouèche, 'L'activité professionnelle des femmes: une ressource, mais pour qui? Une réflexion sur l'accès au divorce', *Sociologie du Travail*, no. 3 (1984), pp. 308–16.
59   Among so many testimonies or observations of experience of the symbolic violence associated with linguistic domination, I shall only cite, for their exemplary character, those offered by Abiodun Goke-Pariola concerning post-independence Nigeria: the perpetuation of an 'internalized denigration of everything native' is seen in a particularly striking way in the relations Nigerians have to their native language (which they will not allow to be taught in schools) and to the language of the former colonizers, which they speak 'adopting the bodily *hexis* of the British . . . so as to produce what is regarded as the British nasal accent' (A. Goke-Pariola, *The Role of Language in the*

masculine domination and feminine submissiveness, which can, without contradiction, be described as both *spontaneous and extorted*, cannot be understood until one takes account of the *durable effects* that the social order exerts on women (and men), that is to say, the dispositions spontaneously attuned to that order which it imposes on them.

Symbolic force is a form of power that is exerted on bodies, directly and as if by magic, without any physical constraint; but this magic works only on the basis of the dispositions deposited, like springs, at the deepest level of the body.[60] If it can act like the release of a spring, that is, with a very weak expenditure of energy, this is because it does no more than trigger the dispositions that the work of inculcation and embodiment has deposited in those who are thereby primed for it. In other words, it finds its conditions of possibility, and its economic equivalent (in an expanded sense of the word 'economic'), in the immense preliminary labour that is needed to bring about a durable transformation of bodies and to produce the permanent dispositions that it triggers and awakens. This transformative action is all the more powerful because it is for the most part exerted invisibly and insidiously through insensible familiarization with a symbolically structured physical world and early, prolonged experience of interactions informed by the structures of domination.

The practical acts of knowledge and recognition of the magical frontier between the dominant and the dominated that are triggered by the magic of symbolic power and through which the dominated, often unwittingly, sometimes unwillingly, contribute to their own domination by tacitly accepting the limits imposed, often take the form of *bodily emotions* – shame, humiliation, timidity, anxiety, guilt – or *passions* and *sentiments* – love, admiration, respect. These emotions are all the more powerful when they are betrayed in visible manifestations such as blushing, stuttering, clumsiness, trembling, anger or impotent

Struggle for Power and Legitimacy, African Studies, no. 31 (Lewiston, N.Y.: Edwin Mellen Press, 1993)).
60   It is possible to understand in these terms the symbolic efficacy of religious messages (Papal bulls, preaching, prophecy, etc.), which is clearly based on previous religious socialization (catechism, church-going and, above all, immersion from an early age in a universe imbued with religiosity).

rage, so many ways of submitting, even despite oneself and 'against the grain' [à son corps défendant], to the dominant judgement, sometimes in internal conflict and division of self, of experiencing the insidious complicity that a body slipping from the control of consciousness and will maintains with the censures inherent in the social structures.

The passions of the dominated habitus (whether dominated in terms of gender, ethnicity, culture or language) – a somatized social relationship, a social law converted into an embodied law – are not of the kind that can be suspended by a simple effort of will, founded on a liberatory awakening of consciousness. If it is quite illusory to believe that symbolic violence can be over-come with the weapons of consciousness and will alone, this is because the effect and conditions of its efficacy are durably and deeply embedded in the body in the form of dispositions. This is seen, in particular, in the case of relations of kinship and all relations built on that model, in which these durable inclina-tions of the socialized body are expressed and experienced in the logic of feeling (filial love, fraternal love, etc.) or duty, which are often merged in the experience of respect and devotion and may live on long after the disappearance of their social condi-tions of production. Thus it is observed that when the external constraints are removed and formal liberties – the right to vote, the right to education, access to all occupations, including politics – are acquired, self-exclusion and 'vocation' (which 'acts' as much negatively as it does positively) take over from explicit exclusion. Exclusion from public places, which, when it is explicitly laid down, as it is among the Kabyles, consigns women to separate spaces and makes approaching a male space, such as the edges of the assembly place, a terrifying ordeal, may elsewhere be achieved almost as effectively through the *socially imposed agoraphobia* which may persist long after the abolition of the most visible taboos and which leads women to exclude themselves from the *agora*.

To point to the marks that domination durably imprints in bodies and the effects it exerts through them does not mean that one is offering support to that particularly vicious way of ratifying domination which consists in making women res-ponsible for their own domination by suggesting, as people sometimes do, that they *choose* to adopt submissive practices ('women are their own worst enemies') or even that they love their own domination, that they 'enjoy' the treatment inflicted on them, in a kind of masochism inherent in their nature. It has to be acknowledged both that the 'submissive' dispositions that are sometimes used to 'blame the victim' are the product of the objective structures, and also that these structures only derive their efficacy from the dispositions which they trigger and which help to reproduce them. Symbolic power cannot be exercised without the contribution of those who undergo it and who only undergo it because they *construct* it as such. But instead of stopping at this statement (as constructivism in its idealist, ethnomethodological or other forms does) one has also to take note of and explain the social construction of the cognitive structures which organize acts of construction of the world and its powers. It then becomes clear that, far from being the conscious, free, deliberate act of an isolated 'subject', this practical construction is itself the effect of a power, durably embedded in the bodies of the dominated in the form of schemes of perception and dispositions (to admire, respect, love, etc.) which *sensitize* them to certain symbolic manifestations of power.

Although it is true that, even when it seems to be based on the brute force of weapons or money, recognition of domination always presupposes an act of knowledge, this does not imply that one is entitled to describe it in the language of consciousness, in an intellectualist and scholastic fallacy which, as in Marx (and above all, those who, from Lukács onwards, have spoken of 'false consciousness'), leads one to expect the liberation of women to come through the immediate effect of the 'raising of consciousness', forgetting – for lack of a dispositional theory of practices – the opacity and inertia that stem from the embedding of social structures in bodies.

Although she shows well the inadequacy of the notion of 'consent' obtained by 'persuasion and seduction', Jeanne Favret-Saada does not really manage to escape from the choice between constraint and consent in the form of 'free acceptance' and 'explicit agreement', because, like Marx, from whom she borrows the language of alienation, she remains enclosed within a philosophy of 'consciousness' (thus she refers to the 'dominated, fragmented, contradictory *con-*

sciousness of the oppressed [woman]' or the 'invasion of women's *consciousness* by the physical, juridical and mental power of men'). Failing to take account of the *durable* effects that the male order exercises on women, she cannot adequately understand the enchanted submission which constitutes the specific effect of symbolic violence.[61] The language of the 'imaginary' which one sees used somewhat recklessly here and there is even more inadequate than that of 'consciousness' in as much as it inclines one in particular to forget that the dominant principle of vision is not a simple mental representation, a fantasy ('ideas in people's heads'), an ideology, but a system of structures durably embedded in things and in bodies. Nicole-Claude Mathieu, in a text entitled 'On the dominated consciousness',[62] has probably gone furthest in the critique of the notion of consent, which 'denies virtually all responsibility on the part of the oppressor',[63] and 'once more casts all the blame on the oppressed';[64] but, because she has not abandoned the language of 'consciousness', she is not quite as radical as she might be in her analysis of *the limitations of the possibilities of thought or action* that domination imposes on the oppressed[65] and 'the invasion of their consciousness by the omnipresent power of men'.[66]

These critical distinctions are not at all gratuitous: they imply that the symbolic revolution called for by the feminist movement cannot be reduced to a simple conversion of consciousnesses and wills. Because the foundation of symbolic violence lies not in mystified consciousnesses that only need to be enlightened but in dispositions attuned to the structure of domination of which they are the product, the relation of complicity that the victims of symbolic domination grant to the

61   J. Favret-Saada, 'L'arraisonnement des femmes', *Les Temps Modernes* (Feb. 1987), pp. 137–50.
62   N.-C. Mathieu, 'De la conscience dominée', in *Catégorisation et idéologies de sexe* (Paris: Côté-femmes, 1991).
63   Ibid., p. 225.
64   Ibid., p. 226.
65   Ibid., p. 216.
66   Ibid., p. 180. It should be noted in passing that the most decisive advances in the critique of the masculine vision of the relations of production (such as the minimization, in discourse and ritual, of the specific contribution of women) have found their most solid support in ethnological analysis of practices, particularly of ritual (cf. the texts brought together by N.-C. Mathieu in N. Echard, O. Journet, C. Michard-Marchal, C. Ribéry, N.-C. Mathieu and N. Tabet, *L'Arraisonnement des femmes. Essais en anthropologie des sexes* (Paris: École des Hautes Études en Sciences Sociales, 1985).

dominant can only be broken through a radical transformation of the social conditions of production of the dispositions that lead the dominated to take the point of view of the dominant on the dominant and on themselves. Symbolic violence is exercised only through an act of knowledge and practical recognition which takes place below the level of the consciousness and will and which gives all its manifestations – injunctions, suggestions, seduction, threats, reproaches, orders or calls to order – their 'hypnotic power'. But a relation of domination that functions only through the complicity of dispositions depends profoundly, *for its perpetuation or transformation*, on the perpetuation or transformation of the structures of which those dispositions are the product (and in particular on the structure of a market in symbolic goods whose fundamental law is that women are treated there as objects which circulate upwards).

Women in the economy of symbolic goods

Thus, dispositions (*habitus*) are inseparable from the structures (*habitudines*, in Leibniz's sense) that produce and reproduce them, in both men and women, and in particular from the whole structure of technical and ritual activities that is ultimately grounded in the structure of the market in symbolic goods.[67] The principle of the inferiority and exclusion of women, which the mythico-ritual system ratifies and amplifies, to the point of making it the principle of division of the whole universe, is nothing other than the fundamental dissymmetry, that of *subject and object, agent and instrument*, which is set up between men and women in the domain of symbolic exchanges, the relations of production and reproduction of symbolic capital, the central device of which is the matrimonial market, and which are the foundation of the whole social order – women can only appear there as objects, or, more precisely, as

---

67 Anticipating some intuitions of modern philosophies, such as that of Peirce, Leibniz speaks of *habitudines*, durable ways of being, structures, resulting from evolution, to designate what is uttered in expression (G. W. Leibniz, 'Quid sit idea', in *Die Philosophische Schriften*, ed. C. I. Gerhardt (Berlin: Weidmannsche Buchhandlung, 1890), vol. 7, pp. 263–4).

symbols whose meaning is constituted outside of them and whose function is to contribute to the perpetuation or expansion of the symbolic capital held by men. The true nature of the status conferred on women is revealed *a contrario* in the limiting case in which, to avoid the extinction of the lineage, a family without a male descendant has no alternative but to *take* for its daughter a man, the *awrith*, who, in contrast to patrilocal custom, comes and lives in his wife's house and who thus circulates like a woman, in other words as an object ('he played the bride,' the Kabyles say). Since masculinity itself is called into question here, both in Béarn and in Kabylia, the whole group grants a kind of arbitrary indulgence to the subterfuges that the humiliated family resorts to in order to save the appearances of its honour and, so far as it is possible, of the 'man-object' who, in abnegating himself as a man, calls into question the honour of the host family.

The explanation of the primacy granted to masculinity in cultural taxonomies lies in the logic of the economy of symbolic exchanges, and more precisely in the social construction of the relations of kinship and marriage alliance which assigns to women their social status as objects of exchange defined in accordance with male interests to help to reproduce the symbolic capital of men. The incest taboo which Lévi-Strauss sees as the act founding society, inasmuch as it entails the necessity of exchange as equal communication between men, is correlative with the institution of the violence through which women are denied as subjects of the exchange and alliance that are set up through them, but by reducing them to the status of objects, or rather, of *symbolic instruments* of male politics. Being condemned to circulate as tokens and thus to institute relations between men, they are reduced to the status of instruments of production or reproduction of symbolic and social capital. And perhaps, to complete the break with Lévi-Strauss's purely 'semiological' view, we should see the circulation of women in de Sade, which, as Anne-Marie Dardigna puts it, 'makes the female body, literally, an assessable, interchangeable object circulating among men like currency',[68] as the disenchanted or

68   A.-M. Dardigna, *Les Châteaux d'Éros ou les infortunes du sexe des femmes* (Paris: Maspero, 1980), p. 88.

cynical limiting case of Lévi-Straussian circulation, made possible by the disenchantment (of which eroticism is one aspect) associated with the generalization of monetary exchanges and displaying overtly the violence on which, in the final analysis, the legitimate circulation of legitimate women is based.

The strictly semiological reading, which conceives the exchange of women as a relation of communication and so masks the *political* dimension of the matrimonial transaction, a symbolic power relation aimed at conserving or expanding symbolic power,[69] and the purely 'economistic' interpretation (Marxist or other) which collapses the logic of the mode of symbolic production into the logic of a mode of strictly economic production and conceives the exchange of women as an exchange of goods both miss the essential ambiguity of the economy of symbolic goods. This economy, oriented towards the accumulation of symbolic capital (honour) transforms various raw materials – above all, women, but more generally any object that can be exchanged with formality – into *gifts* (and not products), that is, communicative signs that are, inseparably, instruments of domination.[70]

Such a theory takes into account not only the specific structure of this exchange, but also the social labour that it requires of those who perform it and above all the labour that is needed to produce and reproduce both its agents (active – men – and passive – women) and its very logic – contrary to the illusion that symbolic capital somehow reproduces itself by its own force, outside of the action of situated and dated agents. To (re)produce the agents is to (re)produce the categories (in both senses – the schemes of perception and appreciation and the social groups) that organize the social world, kinship categories, of course, but also mythico-ritual categories; to (re)produce the

69 On the consequences of the break with the semiological view of exchange in the understanding of linguistic exchange, see Bourdieu, *Ce que parler veut dire*, pp. 13–21 and *passim*.
70 This materialist analysis of the economy of symbolic goods transcends the sterile debate between the 'material' and the 'ideal', perpetuated in the opposition between 'materialist' studies and 'symbolic' studies (which are often quite remarkable, like those of Michele Rosaldo, Sherry Ortner and Gayle Rubin, but are in my view partial: Rosaldo and Ortner have seen the role of symbolic oppositions and the complicity of the dominated; Rubin has seen the link with symbolic exchanges and matrimonial strategies).

game and the stakes is to (re)produce the conditions of access to the social reproduction (and not only to sexuality) that is ensured by an agonistic exchange aimed at accumulating genealogical statuses, the names of lineages or ancestors, in other words symbolic capital, and therefore durable rights and powers over persons. The men produce signs and actively exchange them, as partner-adversaries united by an essential relationship of equality in honour, the very condition of an exchange that can produce inequality in honour, or domination – which is missed by a purely semiological view such as Lévi-Strauss's. There is therefore a radical dissymmetry between man, the subject, and woman, the object of the exchange; between man, who is responsible for and controls production and reproduction, and woman, the *transformed* product of this labour.[71]

When – as is the case in Kabylia – the acquisition of symbolic capital and social capital is more or less the only possible form of accumulation, women are assets which must be protected from offence and suspicion and which, when invested in exchanges, can produce alliances, in other words social capital, and prestigious allies, in other words symbolic capital. To the extent that the value of these alliances, and therefore the symbolic profit they can yield, partly depends on the symbolic value of the women available for exchange, that is to say, on their reputation and especially their chastity – constituted as a fetishized measure of masculine reputation, and therefore of the symbolic capital of the whole lineage – the honour of the brothers or fathers, which induces a vigilance as attentive, and even paranoid, as that of the husbands, is a form of enlightened self-interest.

71 For each of the propositions put forward here, I could (or should) have indicated what distinguishes it on the one hand from Lévi-Strauss's theses (I have done so on just one point, which seemed to me particularly important) and on the other hand from various related analyses, in particular that of Gayle Rubin ('The traffic in women: the political economy of sex', in R. R. Reiter (ed.), *Toward an Anthropology of Women* (New York: Monthly Review Press, 1975)), who, in seeking to account for the oppression of women, picks up some features of Lévi-Strauss's seminal analysis, from a standpoint different from my own. This would have enabled me to do justice to these authors while demonstrating my 'difference', and above all to avoid the risk of seeming to repeat or resurrect analyses to which I am opposed.

The decisive weight of the economy of symbolic goods, which, through the fundamental principle of division, organizes all perception of the social world, weighs on the whole social universe, that is, not only on the economy of economic production, but also on the economy of *biological reproduction*. This explains why it is that, in Kabylia and also in many other traditions, the specifically female work of gestation and childbearing is effaced in favour of the specifically male work of impregnation. (One notes in passing that, although Mary O'Brien, writing from a psychoanalytical perspective, is not wrong to see masculine domination as the product of men's effort to overcome their dispossession from the means of reproduction of the species and to restore the primacy of paternity by disguising the real work of women in childbearing, she fails to relate this 'ideological' work to its true foundations, that is, to the constraints of the economy of symbolic goods, which require biological reproduction to be subordinated to the necessities of the reproduction of symbolic capital.)[72] In the cycle of procreation as in the agrarian cycle, mythico-ritual logic privileges men's intervention, which is always marked, as on the occasion of marriage or the start of ploughing, by public, official, collective rites, at the expense of the periods of gestation, whether that of the earth, in winter, or of woman, which only give rise to optional and almost furtive ritual actions. On the one hand, there is a *discontinuous* and *extra-ordinary* intervention into the course of life, a risky and dangerous action which is performed solemnly – and sometimes, as in the first ploughing, publicly, facing the group; on the other hand, there is a kind of natural and passive process of swelling, of which the woman or the earth is the site, the occasion or the support, rather than the agent, and which requires of the woman only technical or ritual acts of accompaniment, actions that are meant to assist nature in its labour (like hoeing and the gathering of grass for the animals) and are therefore doubly condemned to remain unremarked. Familiar, continuous, ordinary, repetitive and monotonous, this 'humble, easy toil' as the poet puts it[73] is for

72   M. O'Brien, *The Politics of Reproduction* (London: Routledge and Kegan Paul, 1981).
73   P. Verlaine, *Sagesse*, I, viii (*trans.*).

the most part performed out of sight, in the darkness of the house or in the slack periods of the farming year.[74]

The sexual division is inscribed, on the one hand, in the division of productive activities with which we associate the idea of work, and more generally in the division of the labour of maintaining social capital and symbolic capital which gives men the monopoly of all official, public activities, of *representation*, and in particular of all exchanges of honour – exchanges of words (in everyday encounters and above all in the assembly), exchanges of gifts, exchanges of women, exchanges of challenges and murders (of which the limiting case is war). On the other hand, it is inscribed in the dispositions (the habitus) of the protagonists of the economy of symbolic goods – those of women, whom this economy reduces to the state of *objects* of exchange (even if, in certain conditions, they may help, at least by proxy, to orient and organize exchanges, in particular marriages); and those of men, on whom the whole social order, and in particular the positive or negative sanctions associated with the functioning of the market in symbolic goods, lays the obligation to acquire the capacity and propensity, constitutive of the sense of honour, to take seriously all the games thus constituted as serious.

When, as I have done elsewhere,[75] under the heading of the division of labour between the sexes, I described *only the division of productive activities*, I was *mistakenly* adopting an ethnocentric definition of work which I had myself already shown[76] to be a historical invention, profoundly different from the precapitalist definition of 'work' as the exercise of a social function which may be described as 'total' or undifferentiated and which includes activities that modern societies would regard as non-productive, because they have no monetary sanction; this is true – in Kabyle society and in most precapitalist societies, but also in the aristocracy of ancien régime societies, and in the

74 This opposition between the continuous and the discontinuous is also found in modern societies, in the opposition between the routines of women's domestic work and the 'major decisions' that men tend to reserve for themselves (cf. M. Glaude and F. de Singly, 'L'organisation domestique: pouvoir et négociation', *Économie et Statistique* (INSEE, Paris), no. 187 (1986).
75 Bourdieu, *The Logic of Practice*, p. 217.
76 P. Bourdieu, *Travail et travailleurs en Algérie* (Paris and The Hague: Mouton, 1963), and *Algeria 1960* (Paris: Maison des Sciences de l'Homme, and Cambridge: Cambridge University Press, 1979).

privileged classes of capitalist societies – of all practices directly or indirectly oriented towards the reproduction of social capital and symbolic capital, such as negotiating a marriage or speaking in the men's assembly, among the Kabyles, or, elsewhere, playing a smart sport, holding a salon, giving a ball or founding a charitable institution. Such a restricted definition prevents a full understanding of the objective structure of the sexual division of 'tasks' or 'duties', which extends to all domains of practice, and in particular to exchanges, with the difference between public, discontinuous, extra-ordinary male exchanges and private, even secret, continuous, ordinary female exchanges, and to religious or ritual activities, in which similar oppositions are observed.

This primordial investment in the social games (*illusio*), which makes a man a real man – the sense of honour, virility, 'manliness', or, as the Kabyles say, 'Kabylness' (*thakbaylith*) – is the undisputed principle of all the duties towards oneself, the motor or motive of all that a man 'owes to himself', in other words what he must do in order to live up, in his own eyes, to a certain idea of manhood. It is indeed the relationship between a habitus constructed according to the fundamental division of the straight and the curved, the upright and the recumbent, the strong and the weak, in short, the male and the female, and a social space also organized according to this division, that gives rise – as urgent imperatives, things that *must* be done – to the agonistic investments of men, and the virtues, entirely composed of abstention and abstinence, of women.

Thus, the point of honour, that particular form of the sense of the game that is acquired through prolonged submission to the regularities and rules of the economy of symbolic goods, is the principle of the system of reproduction strategies through which men, the holders of the monopoly of the instruments of production and reproduction of symbolic capital, aim to secure the conservation or expansion of this capital – fertility strategies, matrimonial strategies, educational strategies, economic strategies, inheritance strategies, all oriented towards the transmission of inherited powers and privileges.[77] This necessity of

77   On the link between honour and matrimonial and inheritance strategies, see P. Bourdieu, 'Célibat et condition paysanne, *Études rurales*, 5–6 (Apr.–Sept. 1962), pp. 32–126; 'Les stratégies matrimoniales dans le système des stratégies de reproduction', *Annales*, 4–5 (July–Oct. 1972), pp. 1105–27;

the symbolic order, made into a virtue, is the product of the embodiment of the tendency of honour (that is, of the symbolic capital held in common by a lineage or – in the case of Béarn and the noble families of the Middle Ages, and no doubt beyond – by a 'house') to perpetuate itself through the actions of the agents.

Women are excluded from all the public spaces, such as the assembly or the market, where the games ordinarily considered the most serious ones of human existence, such as the games of honour, are played out. Indeed, they are excluded *a priori*, so to speak, in the name of the (tacit) principle of equality in honour, according to which the challenge, because it honours its recipient, is valid only if it is addressed to a man (as opposed to a woman), and a man of honour, capable of providing a riposte which, inasmuch as it too contains a recognition, bestows honour. The perfect circularity of the process indicates that this is an arbitrary assignment.

Manliness and violence

If women, subjected to a labour of socialization which tends to diminish and deny them, learn the negative virtues of self-denial, resignation and silence, men are also prisoners, and insidiously victims, of the dominant representation. Like the dispositions towards submission, those which underlie the pursuit and exercise of domination are not inscribed in a nature, and they have to be learned through a long labour of socialization, in other words, as has been seen, of active differentiation from the opposite sex. Being a man, in the sense of *vir*, implies an ought-to-be, a *virtus*, which imposes itself in the mode of self-evidence, the taken-for-granted. Like nobility, honour – which is inscribed in the body in the form of a set of seemingly natural dispositions, often visible in a particular way of sitting and standing, a tilt of the head, a bearing, a gait, bound up with a way of thinking and acting, an ethos, a belief, etc. –

Y. Castan, *Honnêteté et relations sociales en Languedoc (1715–1780)* (Paris: Plon, 1974), pp. 17–18; R. A. Nye, *Masculinity and Male Codes of Honor in Modern France* (New York: Oxford University Press, 1993).

governs the man of honour, without the need for any external constraint. It *directs* (in both senses) his thoughts and practices like a force (one that can 'carry him away'), but without constraining him mechanically (he may evade the challenge, not rise to its demand); it guides his action like a logical necessity ('he cannot do otherwise' lest he deny himself), but without imposing itself as a rule, or as the implacable logical verdict of a kind of rational calculation. This higher force, which may lead him to accept as inevitable or self-evident, that is, without deliberation or examination, actions which others would see as impossible or unthinkable, is the transcendence of the social that has been made body and which functions as an *amor fati*, love of destiny, the bodily inclination to realize an identity that has been constituted as a social essence and so transformed into a destiny. Nobility, or the point of honour (*nif*), in the sense of the set of dispositions regarded as noble (physical and moral courage, generosity, magnanimity, etc.), is the product of a social labour of nomination and inculcation at the end of which a social identity instituted by one of the 'invisible demarcation lines' laid down by the social world and known and recognized by all inscribes itself in a biological nature and becomes habitus, embodied social law.

Male privilege is also a trap, and it has its negative side in the permanent tension and contention, sometimes verging on the absurd, imposed on every man by the duty to assert his manliness in all circumstances.[78] Inasmuch as its real subject is a collective – the lineage or the house – itself shaped by the demands immanent in the symbolic order, the point of honour presents itself as an ideal, or, more precisely, as a system of demands which inevitably remains, in many cases, inaccessible. *Manli-*

78   And first and foremost, at least in North African societies, his sexual potency, as shown, according to the testimony, recorded in the 1960s, of a pharmacist in Algiers, by men's very frequent and very widespread recourse to aphrodisiacs – always very strongly represented in the armoury of traditional apothecaries. Virility is indeed subject to a more or less masked form of collective judgement, not only at the time of the rites of defloration of the bride, but also through women's conversations, which dwell extensively on sexual matters and lapses in potency. The rush to procure Viagra, both in Europe and the United States, when it first appeared in early 1998, together with many writings by psychotherapists and doctors, shows that anxiety over the physical manifestations of 'manliness' is far from being an exotic peculiarity.

ness, understood as sexual or social reproductive capacity, but also as the capacity to fight and to exercise violence (especially in acts of revenge), is first and foremost a *duty*. Unlike a woman, whose essentially negative honour can only be defended or lost, since her virtue is successively virginity and fidelity, a 'real' man is someone who feels the need to rise to the challenge of the opportunities available to him to increase his honour by pursuing glory and distinction in the public sphere. Exaltation of masculine values has its dark negative side in the fears and anxiety aroused by femininity. Women, weak in themselves and sources of weakness, being the embodiments of the *vulnerability* of honour, of *h'urma*, the sacred of the left hand (female, as opposed to the male sacred of the right hand), and always exposed to offence, are also strong, armed with the weapons of weakness, such as devilish cunning, *thah'raymith*, and magic.[79] Everything thus combines to make the impossible ideal of virility the source of an immense vulnerability. It is this vulnerability which paradoxically leads to sometimes frantic investment in all the masculine games of violence, such as sports in modern societies, and most especially those which most tend to produce the visible signs of masculinity,[80] and to manifest and also test what are called manly virtues, such as combat sports.[81]

79 As has been seen in the myth of origin, in which he discovered with stupor woman's pudenda and the (unreciprocated) pleasure that she revealed to him, man is situated, within the system of oppositions that links him to woman, on the side of good faith and naivety (*niya*), the perfect antitheses of *thah'raymith*.

80 Cf. S. W. Fussell, *Muscle: Confessions of an Unlikely Body Builder* (New York: Poseidon, 1991), and L. Wacquant, 'Why men desire muscles', *Body and Society*, 1, no. 1 (Spring 1995), pp. 163–80. Loïc Wacquant rightly stresses the 'predicament of masculinity' as revealed in body-building, a 'passionate battle, as Barry Glassner calls it, against their own sense of vulnerability', and the 'multisided process through which the masculine *illusio* . . . becomes progressively instilled and inscribed in a particular biological individual' (pp. 171,173).

81 The construction of the traditional Jewish habitus in central Europe, in the late nineteenth century, can be seen as a kind of *perfect inversion* of the process of construction of the male habitus as described here: the explicit refusal of the cult of violence, even in its most ritualized forms, such as duelling or sport, led to a devaluing of physical exercises, especially the most violent ones, in favour of intellectual and spiritual exercises, favouring the development of gentle, 'peaceful' dispositions (confirmed by the rarity of rape and other crimes of violence) (cf. V. Karady, 'Les juifs et la violence stalinienne', *Actes de la Recherche en Sciences Sociales*, no. 120 (Dec. 1997), pp. 3–31).

Like honour – or shame, its reverse side, which we know, in contrast to guilt, is felt *before others* – manliness must be validated by other men, in its reality as actual or potential violence, and certified by recognition of membership of the group of 'real men'. A number of rites of institution, especially in educational or military milieux, include veritable tests of manliness oriented towards the reinforcement of male solidarity. Practices such as some gang rapes – a degraded variant of the group visit to the brothel, so common in the memoirs of bourgeois adolescents – are designed to challenge those under test to prove before others their virility in its violent reality,[82] in other words stripped of all the devirilizing tenderness and gentleness of love, and they dramatically demonstrate the heteronomy of all affirmations of virility, their dependence on the judgement of the male group.

Some forms of 'courage', those demanded or recognized by armies or police forces (and especially the 'elite corps' among them) and gangs of delinquents, but also, in more banal fashion, by some work communities – and which, particularly in the construction industry, for example, encourage or force men to flout safety measures and to deny or defy danger with reckless behaviour that leads to many accidents – spring, paradoxically, from the *fear* of losing the respect or admiration of the group, of 'losing face' in front of one's 'mates' and being relegated to the typically female category of 'wimps', 'girlies', 'fairies', etc. What is called 'courage' is thus often rooted in a kind of cowardice: one has only to think of all the situations in which, to make men kill, torture or rape, the will to dominate, exploit or oppress has relied on the 'manly' fear of being excluded from the world of 'men' without weakness, those who are sometimes called 'tough' because they are tough on their own suffering and more especially on that of others – the assassins, torturers and 'hit men' of all dictatorships and all 'total institutions', even the most ordinary ones, such as prisons, barracks or boarding schools – but also the new 'hatchet men' of modern manage-

82   The link between virility and violence is explicit in the Brazilian tradition, which describes the penis as a *weapon* (R. G. Parker, *Bodies, Pleasures and Passions: Sexual Culture in Contemporary Brazil* (Boston: Beacon Press, 1991), p. 37). There is an equally explicit correlation between penetration (*foder*) and domination (p. 42).

ment, glorified by neoliberal hagiography, who, th
often subject to ordeals of physical courage, manifest t
ity by sacking their superfluous employees. Manliness,
seen, is an eminently *relational* notion, constructed in
and for other men and against femininity, in a kind of *fear* of
the female, firstly in oneself.

2

Anamnesis of the
hidden constants

Ethnological description of a social world that is both sufficiently remote to lend itself more easily to objectification and
entirely constructed around masculine domination acts as a kind
of 'detector' of the infinitesimal traces and scattered fragments
of the androcentric worldview and, consequently, as the instrument of an archaeological history of the unconscious which,
having no doubt been originally constructed in a very ancient
and very archaic state of our societies, inhabits each of us,
whether man or woman. (It is therefore a historical unconscious,
linked not to a biological or psychological nature, like the difference between the sexes according to psychoanalysis, but to a
specifically historical labour of construction – like the labour
which aims to produce the separation of the boy from the
female universe – and one which can consequently be modified
by a transformation of its historical conditions of production.)

So one has to start by extracting everything that knowledge
of the fully developed model of the androcentric 'unconscious'
makes it possible to identify and understand in the manifestations of our own unconscious, which is occasionally glimpsed
in the metaphors of poets or in everyday comparisons so familiar and self-evident that they pass unnoticed. The experience
that an unprepared reader may acquire of the relations of opposition or homology which structure the practices (especially
ritual practices) and representations of Kabyle society – in particular with the aid of the diagram designed to offer a synop-

tic view of them that is totally excluded from native practice –
may range from a sense of self-evidence which, on reflection,
has nothing self-evident about it, and which is based on participation in the same unconscious, to a form of disconcertion,
which may be accompanied by an impression of revelation, or,
more precisely, of *rediscovery*, entirely analogous to that produced by the unexpected necessity of some poetic metaphors.
And the familiarity that he or she may acquire fairly rapidly, as
the ethnologist did, more laboriously, earlier on, with each of
the relations of opposition and with the network of relations of
direct or mediated equivalence which binds each of them to all
the others in a system, thereby conferring on it its *objective and
subjective necessity*, is not the familiarity supplied by the acquisition of a simple knowledge (*savoir*), but the familiarity gained
by that reappropriation of a knowledge (*connaissance*) that is
both possessed and lost from the beginning, which Freud, following Plato, called 'anamnesis'.

But this anamnesis does not apply only to eidetic content, as
it does for Plato; nor only, as it does for Freud, to an individual
process of constitution of the unconscious, the social aspect of
which, without really being excluded, is reduced to a generic
and universal family structure, the embodied imprint of a collective history, which is never socially characterized. It applies
to the phylogeny and ontogeny of an unconscious that is both
collective and individual, the embodied mark of a collective
history and an individual history which imposes on all agents,
both men and women, its system of imperative presuppositions
– of which ethnology constructs the potentially liberatory
axiomatics.

The work of transformation of bodies, which is both sexually
differentiated and sexually differentiating and which is performed partly through the effects of mimetic suggestion, partly
through explicit injunctions and partly through the whole symbolic construction of the view of the biological body (and in
particular the sexual act, conceived as an act of domination,
possession), produces systematically differentiated and differentiating habitus. The masculinization of the male body and the
feminization of the female body, immense and in a sense inter-
minable tasks which, perhaps now more than ever, always
demand a considerable expenditure of time and effort, induce

a somatization of the relation of domination, which is thus naturalized. It is through the training of the body that the most fundamental dispositions are imposed, those which make a person both *inclined and able* to enter into the social games most favourable to the development of manliness – politics, business, science, etc. (Early upbringing encourages boys and girls very unequally to enter into these games, and favours more strongly in boys the various forms of the *libido dominandi* which may find sublimated expressions in the 'purest' forms of the social libido, such as *libido sciendi*.)[1]

Masculinity as nobility

Although the 'ideal' conditions that Kabyle society offered to the androcentric unconscious have largely disappeared and masculine domination has lost part of its immediate self-evidence, some of the mechanisms which underlie this domination continue to function, such as the relation of circular causality that is set up between the objective structures of the social space and the dispositions that they produce in both men and women. The continuous, silent, invisible injunctions that the sexually hierarchized world into which they are thrown addresses to them prepare women, at least as much as explicit calls to order, to accept as self-evident, natural and 'going without saying' arbitrary prescriptions and proscriptions which, inscribed in the order of things, insensibly imprint themselves in the order of bodies.

Although the world always presents itself as strewn with indices and signs designating things to do or not to do, intimating the actions and movements that are possible, probable or impossible, the 'things to do' and 'the things forth-coming' that are offered by a henceforward socially and economically differentiated universe are not addressed to an indifferent agent, a

---

1   One would need to cite all the observations which attest that, from earliest childhood, children are the object of very different *collective expectations* depending on their sex and that, in the scholastic situation, boys receive a privileged treatment (it has been shown that teachers devote more time to them, that they are more often asked questions, less often interrupted, and take a greater part in general discussions).

kind of interchangeable x, but are specified according to the positions and dispositions of each agent. They present themselves as things to be done or things that are not feasible, things that are natural or unthinkable, normal or extraordinary, *for a given category*, i.e. in particular for *a* man or for *a* woman (and of a given social position). The 'collective expectations', as Marcel Mauss would have said, or, in the language of Max Weber, the 'objective potentialities', that social agents discover at every moment have nothing abstract or theoretical about them, even if science must resort to statistics in order to grasp them. They are inscribed in the physiognomy of the familiar environment, in the form of the opposition between the public, masculine universe and private, female worlds, between the public space (the square or the street, the site of all dangers) and the house (it has often been observed that, in advertisements and cartoons, women are, most of the time, placed in the domestic space, in contrast to men, who are rarely associated with the house but fairly often shown in exotic locations), between the places intended primarily for men, such as the bars and clubs of the Anglo-American world, which with their leather upholstery and heavy, dark, angular furniture present an image of hardness and manly toughness, and 'female' spaces, whose pastel shades, knick-knacks, lace or ribbons suggest fragility and frivolity.

It is no doubt in the encounter with the 'objective expectations' inscribed, mostly in the implicit state, in the positions offered to women by the still very strongly sexually differentiated division of labour that the so-called 'feminine' dispositions inculcated by the family and the whole social order are able to be fulfilled or even blossom, and, in this very process, to be rewarded, thereby helping to reinforce the fundamental sexual dichotomy, both in the jobs, which seem to call for submissiveness and the need for security, and in their occupants, who are identified with positions in which, enchanted or alienated, they both find themselves and lose themselves. The essentially social logic of what is called 'vocation' has the effect of producing these kinds of harmonious encounters between dispositions and positions in which the victims of symbolic domination can *felicitously* (in both senses) perform the subaltern or subordinate tasks that are assigned to their virtues of submission, gentleness, docility, devotion and self-denial.

The socially sexed libido enters into communication with the institution which censors or legitimates its expression. 'Vocations' are always in part the more or less fantasmatic anticipation of what the post *promises* (for example, for a secretary, typing documents), and what it *permits* (for example, a relationship of mothering or seduction with the boss). And the encounter with the post may have an effect of revelation inasmuch as, through the explicit or implicit expectations that it contains, it authorizes and favours certain behaviours that are technical and social but also sexual, or sexually marked. Thus the world of work is full of little isolated occupational milieux (a hospital staff, the office of a ministry, etc.) functioning as quasi-families in which the staff manager, almost always a man, exercises a paternalistic authority, based on emotional envelopment or seduction, and, both overburdened with work and taking charge of everything that happens in the institution, offers a generalized protection to a generally female junior staff (nurses, assistants, secretaries) who are thereby encouraged to make an intense, sometimes pathological, investment in the institution and the person who embodies it.

But these objective chances are also recalled in a very concrete and tangible way, not only in all the signs of hierarchy in the division of labour (doctor/nurse, executive/secretary, etc.) but also in all the visible manifestations of the differences between the sexes (bearing, dress, hairstyle) and, more generally, in the seemingly insignificant details of everyday behaviours which contain countless imperceptible calls to order.[2] Thus, in the television studio, women are almost always

---

2   Detailed analysis would be needed of all the social effects of what statistics register as the rate of feminization. It is known, for example, that the prospect of feminization of an occupation reduces its desirability and prestige (cf. J. C. Tonhey, 'Effects of additional women professionals on rating of occupational prestige and desirability', *Journal of Personality and Social Psychology*, 29, no. 1 (1974), pp. 86–9). It is less well known that sex ratio has effects of its own: for example, it favours the acquisition of a set of dispositions which, without being explicitly stipulated in the official syllabus, are inculcated in a diffuse way (cf. M. Duru-Bellat, *L'École des filles. Quelle formation pour quels rôles sociaux* (Paris: L'Harmattan, 1990), p. 27). It has even been observed that girls tend to be less successful in branches of technical education in which they are in a minority (ibid.).

confined to minor roles, variations on the role of 'hostess' traditionally assigned to the 'weaker sex'; even when they are not flanked by a man, for whom they serve as a foil, and who often plays on all the ambiguities implied in the 'couple' relationship, through jokes and more or less subtle allusions, they have difficulty in imposing themselves and what they have to say, and are relegated to a conventional role of 'host' or 'presenter'. When they take part in a public debate, they must fight unceasingly for a chance to speak and to keep attention, and the belittling they suffer is all the more implacable because it is not inspired by any explicit ill-will and is exercised with the perfect innocence of unawareness: men will interrupt them, and, with perfect good faith, address to a man the answer to a perfectly intelligent question just asked by a woman (as if, by definition, such a question could only come from a man). This virtual denial of their existence often forces them to resort to the weapons of the weak, which confirm the stereotypes – an outburst that is inevitably seen as an unjustified whim or as an exhibition that is immediately defined as hysterical; or seduction, which, inasmuch as it is based on a form of recognition of domination, tends to reinforce the established relation of symbolic domination. And one would need to enumerate all the cases in which the best-intentioned of men (for symbolic violence does not operate at the level of conscious intentions) perform discriminatory acts, excluding women, without even thinking about it, from positions of authority, reducing their demands to whims that can be answered with a mollifying word or a tap on the cheek,[3] or, with an apparently opposite intention, reminding them of and in a sense reducing them to their femininity, by drawing attention to their hairstyle or some other physical feature, or using familiar terms of address ('darling', 'dear', etc.) in a formal situation (doctor and patient, for example) – so many infinitesimal 'choices' of the unconscious which come together to help to construct the diminished situation of women and whose cumulative effects are recorded in

3 A number of (female) observers have noted the dissymmetry between men and women in what Nancy Henley calls 'the politics of touching', in other words the ease and frequency of bodily contact (a hand on the cheek, an arm round shoulder or waist, etc.).

the statistics on the very weak representation of women in positions of power, especially economic and political power.

In fact, it is not exaggerated to compare masculinity to a nobility. To be persuaded of this, one only has to observe the double standard, with which the Kabyles are very familiar, applied in the evaluation of male and female activities. Not only can a man not stoop without degrading himself to certain tasks that are socially defined as inferior (not least because it is unthinkable that a man should perform them), but the same tasks may be noble and difficult, when performed by men, or insignificant and imperceptible, easy and futile, when performed by women. As is seen in the difference between the chef and the cook, the couturier and the seamstress, a reputedly female task only has to be taken over by a man and performed outside the private sphere in order for it to be thereby ennobled and transfigured: 'Work', as Margaret Maruani observes, 'is always different depending on whether it is performed by men or by women.' If the statistics establish that so-called skilled (*qualifiés*) jobs are more often held by men whereas the work assigned to women is more often 'unqualified', this is partly because every job, whatever it may be, is in a sense qualified by being performed by men (who, in this respect, are all, by definition, of 'quality').[4] Thus, just as the most perfect mastery of fencing could not open the doors of the *noblesse d'épée* to a commoner, so 'keyboard operators' (*clavistes*), whose entry into the publishing trades aroused formidable resistance on the part of men, who saw a threat to their occupational mythology of highly skilled labour, were not recognized as performing the same *trade* (*métier*) as their male colleagues, from whom they are separated by a simple curtain, although they perform the same *labour*: 'Whatever they do, *clavistes* are typists and have no qualification. Whatever they do, the *correcteurs* are professionals of the publishing world and are therefore highly skilled.'[5] And after long struggles by women for recognition of their skills, the tasks that technological changes had radically redistributed between men and

---

4   M. Maruani and C. Nicole, *Au Labeur des dames. Métiers masculins, emplois féminins* (Paris: Syros/Alternatives, 1989), p. 15.
5   Ibid., pp. 34–77.

women were arbitrarily redefined so as to impoverish women's work while maintaining the superior value of men's work.[6] It can be seen that the Kabyle principle that the work of a woman is condemned to remain invisible – she is expected to labour all day in the house, 'like a fly in the whey; outside the house, nothing of her work is seen'[7] – continues to apply in a seemingly very different context, as is shown by the fact that women are still very commonly denied the hierarchical title corresponding to their real work.

'Collective expectations', positive or negative, through the subjective expectations that they impose, tend to inscribe themselves in bodies in the form of permanent dispositions. Thus, by virtue of the universal law of the adjustment of expectations to chances, aspirations to possibilities, prolonged and invisibly diminished experience that is sexually characterized through and through tends, by discouraging it, to undermine even the inclination to perform acts that are not expected of women – without them even being denied to them. As is shown clearly by this testimony on the changes in dispositions following a change of sex, it favours the appearance of a 'learned helplessness': 'The more I was treated as a woman, the more woman I became. I adapted willy-nilly. If I was assumed to be incompetent at reversing cars, or opening bottles, oddly incompetent I felt myself becoming. If a case was thought too heavy for me, I found it so myself.'[8] This is a magnificent evocation, made possible by comparison, of the kind of reverse or negative Pygmalion effect that is exerted so early and so continuously on women that it ends up being completely unnoticed (I am thinking, for example, of the way in which parents, teachers and fellow pupils discourage – or, one might say, 'non-encourage' – girls from choosing certain subjects, especially scientific and

6 Perpetuation of arbitrary differences can be based on the most archaic divisions of the mythic worldview, between hot and cold, for example, as is seen in the glass industry, where there is a division between the hot sector (the foundry, the site of manufacture), which is male and regarded as noble, and the cold sector (inspection, sorting, packaging), which is less noble and left to women (H. Sumiko Hirata, *Paradigmes d'organisation industriels et rapports sociaux. Comparaison Brésil–France–Japon* (Paris: IRESCO, 1992).
7 P. Bourdieu, *The Logic of Practice* (Cambridge: Polity, 1990), p. 276.
8 J. Morris, *Conundrum* (New York: Harcourt, Brace, Jovanovich, 1974), pp. 165–6.

technical ones: 'The teachers always tell us we have less stamina, and . . . we end up believing it.' 'They constantly tell us the sciences are easier for boys. So, naturally . . .') And it is understandable, in terms of this logic, that 'chivalrous' protection itself may not only lead to their confinement or serve to justify it, but can help to keep women away from all contact with all the aspects of the real world 'for which they are not made' because those things are not made for women.

All the calls to order inscribed in the order of things, all the silent injunctions or muted threats inherent in the normal course of the world are, of course, specified according to the particular fields, and the difference between the sexes presents itself to women, in each field, in specific forms, through for example the *dominant definition of practice* that prevails within it and which no one would think of seeing as sexed and therefore open to question. The particularity of the dominant is that they are in a position to ensure that their particular way of being is recognized as universal. The definition of excellence is in any case charged with masculine implications that have the particularity of not appearing as such. The definition of a post, especially one of authority, includes all kinds of sexually characterized abilities and aptitudes: if so many positions are so difficult for women to occupy, it is because they are tailor-made for men whose manliness is itself constructed by opposition to women as they are today. To succeed completely in holding a position, a woman would need to possess not only what is explicitly demanded by the job description, but also a whole set of properties which the male occupants normally bring to the job – a physical stature, a voice, or dispositions such as aggressiveness, self-assurance, 'role distance', what is called natural authority, etc., for which men have been tacitly prepared and trained as men.

In other words, the norms by which women are measured are in no way universal. What is called *universalist* feminism, because it ignores the effect of domination and all that the apparent universality of the dominant owes to his relation to the dominated – here, everything concerned with manliness – inscribes in the universal definition of the human being historical properties of the manly man, constructed in opposition to women. But what is called *differentialist* feminism, because it too ignores what the dominant definition owes to the historical relation of domination and to the pursuit of difference that is constitutive of it (what is manliness, ultimately, but a non-femininity?), equally does not escape a gentle form of essentialism in its concern to enhance the value of female experience: just as *negritude* as advocated by Senghor accepted some features of the dominant definition of the black, such as sensitivity, so too this feminism forgets that the 'difference' only appears when one adopts the point of view of the dominant on the dominated and that precisely that from which it seeks to differentiate itself (for example, by exalting, as Chodorow does, *relatedness* in opposition to masculine *separatedness*, or, like some advocates of women's writing, a particular relation to the body) is the product of a historical relation of differentiation.

Female being as being-perceived

Everything in the genesis of the female habitus and in the social conditions of its actualization combines to make the female experience of the body the limiting case of the universal experience of the body-for-others, constantly exposed to the objectification performed by the gaze and the discourse of others. The relation to one's own body cannot be reduced to a 'body image', in other words the subjective representation ('self-image' or 'looking-glass self'), associated with a certain degree of 'self-esteem', that an agent has of his or her social effects (seductiveness, charm, etc.) and which is largely built up from the objective representation of the body, descriptive or normative 'feedback' supplied by others (parents, peers, etc.). Such a model forgets that the whole social structure is present at the heart of the interaction, in the form of schemes of perception and appreciation inscribed in the bodies of the interacting agents. These schemes, in which a group embeds its fundamental structures (as big/small, strong/weak, coarse/fine, etc.), are interposed from the outset between every agent and his or her body, because the reactions or representations that one's body gives rise to in others and one's own perception of those reactions are themselves constructed according to those schemes. A reaction produced on the basis of the oppositions big/small and male/female (like all judgements of the type 'she's too tall for a girl', or 'it's a shame, in a girl', or 'it doesn't matter so much in a boy', a variant of the Kabyle saying, 'There are no faults for a man') is an opportunity to acquire the schemes concerned, which, when turned by the subject herself on her own body, will produce the same reaction, and to feel the practical experience of the body that they induce.

Thus, the perceived body is socially doubly determined. On the one hand, in even its seemingly most natural aspects (its volume, height, weight, musculature, etc.) it is a social product that depends on its social conditions of production through various mediations, such as working conditions (especially as regards the associated deformations and occupational diseases) and eating habits. Bodily *hexis*, which includes both the strictly physical shape of the body ('physique') and the way it is 'carried', deportment, bearing, is assumed to express the 'deep being', the true 'nature' of the 'person', in accordance with the postulate of the correspondence between the 'physical' and the 'moral' which gives rise to the practical or rationalized knowledge whereby 'psychological' and 'moral' properties are associated with bodily or physiognomic indices (e.g. a thin, sleek body tends to be perceived as the sign of a manly control of bodily appetites). But this language of nature, which is supposed to reveal both what is most hidden and what is most true, is in fact a language of social identity, thereby naturalized, in the form for example of 'vulgarity' and what is called 'natural distinction'.

On the other hand, these bodily properties are apprehended through schemes of perception whose use in acts of evaluation depends on the position occupied in social space: the prevailing taxonomies tend to oppose and hierarchize those properties most frequent among the dominant and those most frequent among the dominated (thin/fat, big/small, elegant/coarse, delicate/gross, etc.).[9] The social representation of his or

9   Dominique Merllié has brought to light a similar mechanism by analysing the differential perception that boys and girls have of the difference between male and female handwriting (cf. D. Merllié, 'Le sexe de l'écriture. Note sur la perception sociale de la féminité', *Actes de la Recherche en Sciences Sociales*, 83 (June 1990), pp. 40–51).

her body, which every agent has to reckon with, probably from a very early age, is thus obtained by the application of a social taxonomy whose principle is the same as that of the bodies to which it is applied.[10] Thus, the gaze is not a simple universal and abstract power to objectify, as Sartre maintained: it is a symbolic power whose efficacy depends on the relative position of the perceiver and the perceived and on the degree to which the schemes of perception and appreciation that are brought into play are known and recognized by the person to whom they are applied.

The practical experience of the body, which is generated in the application to one's own body of the fundamental schemes springing from embodiment of the social structures and which is continuously reinforced by the reactions, generated by the same schemes, that one's own body produces in others, is one of the principles of the construction in each agent of a durable relation to his or her own body. This particular way of bearing the body, of presenting it to others, expresses, above all, the distance between the body as practically experienced and the legitimate body, and, by the same token, a practical anticipation of the chances of success of interactions which helps to define those chances (through features commonly described as assurance, self-confidence, ease, etc.). The probability of experiencing the body with embarrassment (the form par excellence of the experience of the 'alienated body'), malaise, timidity or shame rises with the discrepancy between the socially demanded body and the practical relation to the body that is imposed by the gazes and reactions of others. It varies very strongly according to sex and position in the social space. Thus, the opposition between big and small, which, as a number of experiments have shown, is one of the fundamental principles of the experience that agents have of their bodies and of all the practical use that they

10 Thus bodies would have every chance of being valued strictly in accordance with the positions of their owners in the social space if the autonomy of the logic of biological heredity did not sometimes, and exceptionally, bestow on the economically and socially most deprived the rarest bodily properties, such as beauty (which is then called 'fatal' because it threatens the established order), and if, conversely, the accidents of genetics did not sometimes deprive the 'great' of the bodily attributes of their position such as beauty or height.

make of it, in particular the place they assign to it[11] (the common representation which gives the man the dominant position, that of the protector who enfolds, watches over, looks down from above, etc.[12]), is specified between the sexes, which are themselves conceived through this opposition. In accordance with a logic that is also seen at work in the relation between dominated and dominant within the social space, and which leads each side to apply the same opposition, but *giving opposite values to the terms that it opposes*, Seymour Fisher observes that men tend to be dissatisfied with parts of their bodies that they judge 'too small' whereas women tend to be critical of parts of their bodies that they judge 'too big'.

Masculine domination, which constitutes women as symbolic objects whose being (*esse*) is a being-perceived (*percipi*), has the effect of keeping them in a permanent state of bodily insecurity, or more precisely of symbolic dependence. They exist first through and for the gaze of others, that is, as welcoming, attractive and available *objects*. They are expected to be 'feminine', that is to say, smiling, friendly, attentive, submissive, demure, restrained, self-effacing. And what is called 'femininity' is often nothing other than a form of indulgence towards real or supposed male expectations, particularly as regards the aggrandizement of the ego. As a consequence, dependence on others (and not only men) tends to become constitutive of their being.

This *heteronomy* is the principle of dispositions such as the desire to draw attention and to please, sometimes perceived as coquettishness, or the propensity to expect a great deal from love, which, as Sartre says, is the only thing capable of providing the feeling of being justified in the particularities of one's being, starting with one's body.[13] Continuously under the gaze

---

11   Cf. on this point S. Fisher and C. E. Cleveland, *Body Image and Personality* (Princeton and New York: Van Nostrand, 1958).
12   On the relation of protective enfolding as expressed in advertising, cf. E. Goffman, 'The ritualization of subordination', in *Gender Advertisements* (London: Macmillan, 1979), pp. 40–56.
13   If women are particularly inclined to what is called romantic love this is no doubt partly because they have a particular self-interest in it: not only does it promise to free them from masculine domination, but, both in its most ordinary form, with marriage, in which, in male societies, women circulate upwards, and in its extra-ordinary forms, it also offers them a route, sometimes the only one, to upward social mobility.

of others, women are condemned constantly to experience the discrepancy between the real body to which they are bound and the ideal body towards which they endlessly strive.[14] Needing the gaze of others to constitute themselves, they are continuously oriented in their practice by the anticipated evaluation of the price that their bodily appearance, their way of bearing and presenting it, may receive (hence the more or less marked propensity to self-denigration and to the embodiment of social judgement in the form of physical embarrassment and timidity).

It is in the petite bourgeoisie, which, because of its position in the social space, is particularly exposed to all the effects of anxiety about the social gaze, that women reach the extreme form of symbolic alienation. (In other words the effects of social position may in some cases, as they do here, reinforce the effects of gender, or in other cases attenuate them, without, it seems, ever eliminating them.) By contrast, intensive practice of a sport leads to a profound transformation of the subjective and objective experience of the body. It no longer exists only for others or, which amounts to the same thing, for the mirror (an instrument with which one can not only see oneself but try to see how one is seen and endeavour to make oneself look as one wishes to be seen); it is no longer merely a thing that is made to be looked at or which one has to look at in order to prepare it to be looked at. Instead of being a body for others it becomes a body for oneself; the passive body becomes an active and acting body. In the eyes of men, however, those women who break the tacit relation of availability and in a sense reappropriate their body image, and with it their body, appear as 'unfeminine', even lesbian – the affirmation of intellectual independence, which also reveals itself in bodily manifestations, produces entirely similar effects.[15] More generally, access to power of any kind places women in a 'double bind': if they behave like men, they risk losing the obligatory attributes of 'femininity' and call into question the natural right of men to the positions of power; if they behave

---

14   Cosmetic treatments, which absorb much time, money and energy (differentially between the classes), encounter their limiting case in cosmetic surgery, which has become a vast industry in the United States (with a million and a half clients a year – cf. S. Bordo, *Unbearable Weight: Feminism, Western Culture and the Body* (Berkeley: University of California Press, 1993), p. 25).
15   Cf. C. A. MacKinnon, *Feminism Unmodified: Discourses on Life and Law* (Cambridge, Mass.: Harvard University Press, 1987), pp. 121ff.

like women, they appear incapable and unfit for the job. These contradictory expectations simply take over from those to which they are structurally exposed as objects offered on the market in symbolic goods, simultaneously invited to use all means to please and charm and expected to repel the seductive manoeuvres that this kind of submission in advance to the verdict of the male gaze may seem to have provoked. This contradictory combination of openness and closedness, restraint and seduction, is all the more difficult to achieve because it is subject to the appreciation of men, who may make unconscious or self-interested errors of interpretation. Thus, as one female informant pointed out, faced with men's sexual jokes, women often have no other choice than to exclude themselves or participate, at least passively, in order to try to integrate themselves, but then running the risk of no longer being able to protest if they are victims of sexism or sexual harassment.

Sandra Lee Bartky, who gives an extremely perceptive description of the female experience of the body, is wrong, it seems to me, to attribute the inculcation in women of 'profound anxieties about their bodies' and 'an acute sense of their physical unworthiness' solely to the pressure of the 'fashion–beauty complex'.[16] The influence of these institutions is undeniable, but they do no more than reinforce the effect of the fundamental relationship instituting women in the position of a being-perceived condemned to perceive itself through the dominant, i.e. masculine, categories. And to understand the 'masochistic dimension' of female desire, in other words the 'eroticization of social relations of domination'[17] ('for many women, dominance in men is exciting,' as Bartky puts it[18]), one has to hypothesize that women look to men (and also, but secondarily, to the 'fashion–beauty complex') for subterfuges to reduce their 'sense of physical inadequacy'; and it can be assumed that the gaze of the powerful, which carries authority, especially among other men, is particularly able to fulfil this function of reassurance.[19]

16   S. Lee Bartky, *Femininity and Domination: Studies in the Phenomenology of Oppression* (New York and London: Routledge, 1990), p. 41.
17   Ibid., p. 51.
18   Ibid., p. 51 and also p. 47.
19   In particular, the dominant agent has the power to impose his own vision of himself as objective and collective (the limiting case being represented by equestrian statues or official portraits), to make other people abdicate their

The female vision of the male vision

The structure imposes its constraints on the two terms of the relationship of domination, and therefore on the dominant themselves, who can benefit from it while being, in Marx's phrase, 'dominated by their domination'. And this is because, as is shown well enough by all the games associated with the opposition between the big and the small, the dominant cannot fail to apply to themselves, that is, to their bodies and to everything they are and do, the schemes of the unconscious, which, in their case, give rise to formidable demands – as is sensed, and tacitly recognized, by the women who do not want a husband smaller than themselves. And so one has to analyse, in its contradictions, the masculine experience of domination, turning for this purpose to Virginia Woolf – not so much to the author of those endlessly quoted classics of feminism, *A Room of One's Own* and *Three Guineas*, as to the novelist, the author of *To the Lighthouse*, who, no doubt aided by the anamnesis favoured by the work of writing,[20] presents an evocation of the relations between the sexes freed from all the clichés on sex, money and power that still persist in her more theoretical texts. For in the background of this narrative one finds an incomparably lucid evocation of the female gaze, which is itself particularly lucid on the desperate, and in its triumphant unawareness somewhat tragic, effort that every man has to make to rise to his own childhood conception of manhood.

This concerned and indulgent lucidity is evoked right from the start of the novel. It is probable that, unlike Mrs Ramsay, who fears that her husband has been overheard, most readers, especially male ones, do not understand or even notice the strange and even ridiculous situation in which Mr Ramsay has

generic capacity to objectify, as in love or belief, and he thus constitutes himself as an absolute subject, with no exterior, fully justified in existing as he exists.

20   Virginia Woolf was aware of the paradox, which will surprise only those who have a simplistic view of literature and its ways of truth-telling: 'I prefer, where truth is important, to write fiction' (V. Woolf, *The Pargiters* (New York: Harcourt, Brace, Jovanovich, 1977), p. 9). Or again: 'Fiction here is likely to contain more truth than fact' (V. Woolf, *A Room of One's Own* (London: Hogarth, 1929), p. 7).

put himself: 'Suddenly a loud cry, as of a sleep-walker, half roused, something about "Stormed at with shot and shell" sung out with the utmost intensity in her ear, made her turn apprehensively to see if anyone heard him.'[21] And it is also likely that they understand no better when, a few pages later, Mr Ramsay is overheard by other characters, Lily Briscoe and her friend. Only slowly, through the various visions that different characters have of it, will they understand Mr Ramsay's behaviour and his wife's anxiety about it: 'And his habit of talking aloud, or saying poetry aloud, was growing on him, she was afraid; for sometimes it was awkward . . .'[22] The same Mr Ramsay who, from the first page of the novel, had appeared as an imposing masculine character, is caught behaving like a child.

The whole logic of the character lies in this seeming contradiction. Mr Ramsay, like the ancient king discussed by Benveniste in *Indo-European Language and Society*, is a man whose words are *verdicts*; a man who in one sentence can wipe out the 'extraordinary joy' of his son James, who is entirely focused on the next day's expedition to the lighthouse ('"But," said his father, stopping in front of the drawing-room window, "it won't be fine."'). His predictions are self-fulfilling, they make themselves true – either because they act as orders, blessings or curses which magically bring about what they state, or because, much more terrifyingly, they simply state magically what is foretold in signs accessible only to the insight of the quasi-divine visionary, who can interpret the world, redouble the force of the laws of natural or social nature by converting them into laws of reason and experience, rational and reasonable statements of science and wisdom. The imperative utterance of paternal prophecy is both a forecast of science, which sends the future into the past, and a prediction of wisdom which gives to that still unreal future the sanction of experience and of the absolute conformism that it implies.

It is mainly through the agent who holds the monopoly of the legitimate exercise of symbolic violence (and not only of

---

21   V. Woolf, *To the Lighthouse* (Harmondsworth: Penguin, 1964), p. 20. It only gradually becomes clear to the reader that Mr Ramsay, a teacher surrounded by pupils and colleagues, is overheard reciting Tennyson's *Charge of the Light Brigade*.
22   Ibid., p. 82.

sexual potency) within the family that the psychosomatic action is performed which leads to the somatization of the law. The words of the father have a magical effect of constitution, creative naming, because they speak directly to the body, which, as Freud pointed out, takes metaphors literally; and if 'vocations' generally seem so astonishingly well adapted to the places actually available (according to sex, but also birth rank and many other variables), this is no doubt largely due to the fact that, even when they seem to stem from nothing other than the arbitrariness of free will, the words and judgements of the *paterna potestas* which play a large part in shaping them emanate from a personage himself shaped by and for the censures of necessity and consequently led to have the reality principle as pleasure principle.

The implacable words of the father, an unconditional alignment on the order of things, are opposed to maternal comprehension, which answers the paternal verdict with a questioning of necessity and an affirmation of contingency based on a pure act of faith – ' "But it *may* be fine – I *expect* it will be fine" '[23] – and which acknowledges the self-evident law of desire and pleasure but makes a twofold conditional concession to the reality principle: ' "Yes, of course, if it's fine tomorrow," said Mrs Ramsay. "But you'll have to be up with the lark," she added.' The father's *no* does not need to be uttered, or to justify itself: for a reasonable being ('Be reasonable', 'Later you will understand'), there is no choice but silent acceptance of the inevitability of things. The word of the father is never more terrible in its pitiless solicitude than when it adopts the logic of prophylactic prediction, which announces the future that is feared only in order to exorcize it ('You'll come to a bad end', 'You will bring shame on all of us', 'You'll never pass your exams', etc.) and whose confirmation by the facts offers the occasion for retrospective triumph ('I told you so'), a disenchanted compensation for the suffering caused by the disappointment of not having been proved wrong.

It is this kill-joy realism, complicit with the order of the world, that triggers the hatred of the father, a hatred directed, as in adolescent revolt, not so much against the necessity that

23 Ibid., p. 7.

the paternal discourse claims to unveil as against the arbitrary acceptance that the all-powerful father grants it, thereby proving his weakness: 'Had there been an axe handy, a poker, or any weapon that would have gashed a hole in his father's breast and killed him, there and then, James would have seized it. Such were the extremes of emotion that Mr Ramsay excited in his children's breast by his mere presence; standing, as now, *lean* as a *knife*, *narrow* as the *blade* of one, grinning sarcastically, not only with the pleasure of disillusioning his son and casting ridicule upon his wife, who was ten thousand times better in every way than he was (James thought), but also with some secret conceit at his own *accuracy* of judgement.'[24] The most radical revolts of childhood and adolescence are perhaps turned not so much against the father as against the submission spontaneously granted to the submissive father, against the primary instinct to obey him and accept his reasoning.

At this point, with the aid of the indeterminacy of indirect free speech, we move insensibly from the children's point of view on the father to the father's point of view on himself. This point of view strictly has nothing personal about it since, as the dominant, legitimate point of view, it is nothing other than the high estimation that the man who aims to realize in his being the ought-to-be that the social world assigns to him – the ideal of the man and father he *must* be – can and must have of himself: 'What he said was true. It was always true. He was incapable of untruth; never tampered with a fact; never altered a disagreeable word to suit the pleasure or convenience of any mortal being, least of all his own children, who, sprung from his loins, should be aware from childhood that life is difficult; facts uncompromising; and the passage to that fabled land where our brightest hopes are extinguished, our frail barks founder in darkness (here Mr Ramsay would *straighten his back* and narrow his little blue *eyes upon the horizon*), one that needs, above all, courage, truth, and the power to endure.'[25]

Seen from this angle, Mr Ramsay's gratuitous harshness is no longer the effect of an impulse as egoistic as the pleasure of disillusioning. It is the free affirmation of a choice, that of

24   Ibid., p. 6 (my italics).
25   Ibid. (my italics).

uprightness and also of enlightened paternal love, which, refusing to give way to the culpable facility of a female, and blindly maternal, indulgence, feels called upon to express the pitiless necessity of the world. This is probably what is meant by the metaphor of the knife and the blade, which the naively Freudian interpretation would flatten, and which, as among the Kabyles, situates the masculine role – for once the word and the theatrical metaphor are appropriate – on the side of the knife, of violence and murder, that is, on the side of a cultural order built up against the original fusion with the maternal nature and against surrender to indulgence, the instinct and impulses of female nature. One begins to suspect that the executioner is also a victim, and that the word of the father is liable, because of its very power, to convert the probable into destiny.

This feeling can only intensify when it is discovered that the inflexible father who, in a sentence that brooks no argument, has destroyed his son's dreams has been caught playing like a child, offering to those who 'had encroached upon a privacy', Lily Briscoe and her friend, 'a thing they had not been meant to see'[26] – the fantasies of the *libido academica* which express themselves in warlike games. But one must quote in full the long reverie which *The Charge of the Light Brigade* inspires in Mr Ramsay, in which the evocation of soldierly valour – the charge into the valley of death, the lost battle, the heroism of the leader ('Yet he would not die *lying down*; he would find some crag of rock, and there, his *eyes fixed* on the storm . . . he would *die standing*.') – is intermingled with anxious thoughts of the posthumous fate of the philosopher ('Z is only reached once by one man in a generation.' 'He would never reach R.'): 'How many men in a thousand million, he asked himself, reach Z after all? Surely the leader of a forlorn hope may ask himself that, and answer without treachery to the expedition behind him, "One perhaps". *One in a generation*. Is he to be blamed then if he is not that one? Provided he has toiled honestly, given to the best of his power, till he has no more left to give? And *his fame* lasts how long? It is permissible even for a dying hero to think before he dies how men will speak of him hereafter.

26 Ibid., p. 22.

His fame lasts perhaps two thousand years. . . . Who then could blame the leader of that forlorn party which after all has climbed *high enough* to see the waste of the years and the perishing of stars, if before death stiffens his limbs beyond the power of movement he does a little consciously raise his numbed fingers to his *brow*, and *square his shoulders*, so that when the search party comes they will find him dead at his post, the *fine figure of a soldier?* Mr Ramsay *squared his shoulders* and stood *very upright* by the urn. Who shall blame him, if, so standing for a moment, he dwells upon *fame*, upon search parties, upon *cairns* raised by *grateful followers* over his bones? Finally, who shall blame the leader of the doomed expedition, if . . .'[27]

The 'fade-in fade-out' technique, much favoured by Virginia Woolf, works wonders here. Because warlike adventure and the glory which consecrates it are a metaphor for intellectual adventure and the symbolic capital of celebrity that it pursues, the ludic *illusio* makes it possible to reproduce at a higher degree of derealization, and therefore at lower cost, the academic *illusio* of ordinary existence, with its vital stakes and passionate investments – everything that drives the arguments of Mr Ramsay and his disciples. It allows the partial, controlled work of disinvestment that is needed in order to absorb and overcome disillusionment ('He had not genius; he laid no claim to that'[28]), while saving the fundamental *illusio*, the investment in the game itself, the conviction that the game is worth playing all the same, right to the end, and according to the rules (since, after all, the humblest private can at least 'die standing' . . .). This visceral investment, the expression of which is essentially *postural*, is performed through poses, positions or gestures which are all oriented in the direction of uprightness, rectitude, the raising of the body or its symbolic substitutes, the cairn or the statue.

The original *illusio*, which is constitutive of masculinity, is no doubt at the basis of the *libido dominandi* in all the specific

---

27 Ibid., pp. 41–2 (my italics). This evocation of the *libido academica*, which may be expressed under the cover of literary neutralization, could be added in support of the analyses of the academic field presented in *Homo Academicus* (Cambridge: Polity, 1996).
28 Ibid., p. 41.

forms it takes in the different fields.[29] It is what causes men (as opposed to women) to be socially instituted and instructed in such a way that they let themselves be caught up, like children, in all the games that are socially assigned to them, of which the form par excellence is war. Allowing himself to be overheard in a daydream which betrays the puerile vanity of his deepest investments, Mr Ramsay abruptly reveals that the games to which he devotes himself, like other men, are children's games – which are not seen for what they are because, precisely, the *collective collusion* endows them with the necessity and reality of shared self-evidences. The fact that, among the games that are constitutive of social existence, those that are called serious are reserved for men, whereas women are confined to children and childish things ('without replying, dazed and blinded, she bent her head. . . . There was nothing to be said.'[30]), helps to mask the fact that a man is also a child playing at being a man. Generic alienation is the basis of the specific privilege: it is because men are trained to recognize social games in which the stake is some form of domination and are designated very early, in particular by the rites of institution, as dominant, and thereby endowed with the *libido dominandi*, that they have the double-edged privilege of indulging in the games of domination.

On their side, women have the *entirely negative* privilege of not being taken in by the games in which privileges are fought for and, for the most part, of not being caught up in them, at least directly, in the first person. They can even see the vanity of them, and so long as they are not vicariously engaged in them, look with amused indulgence on the desperate efforts of the 'child-man' to play the man and the childish despair into which his failures cast him. They can watch the most serious games from the distant standpoint of the spectator who watches the storm from the shore – which can lead them to be seen as frivolous and incapable of taking an interest in serious things, such as politics. But because this distance is an effect of domination, they are almost always condemned to participate,

29   On this point, see P. Bourdieu, *Pascalian Meditations* (Cambridge: Polity, 2000), p. 164ff.
30   *To the Lighthouse*, p. 38.

out of an affective solidarity with the player which does not
imply a genuine intellectual and affective participation in the
game and which often makes them unconditional supporters
who nonetheless know little of the reality of the game and its
stakes.[31]

Thus Mrs Ramsay understands immediately the embarrassing situation into which her husband has put himself by
declaiming *The Charge of the Light Brigade*. She fears for his sake
not so much what he may be suffering from being overheard
as the suffering that lies behind his aberration. Everything in
her behaviour shows this when, wounded and reduced to the
over-grown child he is, the severe father, who has just indulged
in his (compensatory) taste for 'disillusioning his son and ridi-
culing his wife',[32] comes and seeks her sympathy for suffering
that springs from the *illusio* and disillusionment: 'She stroked
James's head; she transferred to him what she felt for her
husband.'[33] Through one of the condensations that the logic of
practice allows, in a gesture of emotional protection for which
her whole social being has destined and prepared her,[34] Mrs
Ramsay identifies the little man who has just discovered the
unbearable negativity of the real and the adult who consents to
reveal the full extent of the seemingly disproportionate disar-
ray into which his 'disaster' has thrown him. By explicitly men-
tioning his verdict on the trip to the lighthouse and asking his
wife's forgiveness for the brutality with which he pronounced
it (he 'rather sheepishly prodded his son's bare legs'; he offers
'very humbly' to go and ask the coastguards for their opinion),
Mr Ramsay reveals very clearly that the rebuff is linked to the
embarrassing scene and with the game of *illusio* and disillusionment.[35] Although she is careful to conceal her insight, no

31   This is particularly seen in the way young working-class women share in
the sporting passions of 'their men' – a participation which, because of its
arbitrary and affective character, can only strike the latter as frivolous, even
absurd, as does the opposite attitude, more common after marriage, of jealous
hostility towards a passion for things from which they are excluded.
32   *To the Lighthouse*, p. 43.
33   Ibid., p. 36.
34   Mrs Ramsay's protective function is evoked several times, notably
through the metaphor of the hen which flaps its wings to protect its chicks
(ibid., pp. 25, 26, 27): 'she had the whole of the other sex under her protection; for reasons she could not explain' (p. 9, my italics, and also p. 45).
35   Ibid., p. 38.

doubt to protect her husband's dignity, Mrs Ramsay knows very well that the pitiless verdict comes from a pitiful being who is himself a victim of the inexorable verdicts of the real and himself needs pity – we discover later that she knew perfectly well the weak point where her husband could be hurt at any time: ' "Ah, but how long do you think it'll last?" said somebody. It was as if she had antennae trembling out from her, which, intercepting certain sentences, forced them upon her attention. This was one of them. She scented danger for her husband. A question like that would lead, almost certainly, to something being said which reminded him of his own failure. How long would he be read – he would think at once.'[36] But perhaps she thus succumbs to an ultimate strategy, that of the unhappy man who, by playing the child, is sure to awaken the dispositions of maternal compassion that are assigned to women.[37]

One would need to quote here the extraordinary oblique dialogue in which Mrs Ramsay continuously humours her husband, first by accepting the apparent object of the domestic dispute, instead of pointing out, for example, the disproportion between his anger and its declared cause. Each apparently anodyne sentence of the two speakers involves much larger, more fundamental stakes, and each of the two partner-adversaries knows this because of their intimate and quasi-perfect knowledge of the other, which, at the price of a minimum complicity in bad faith, allows them to engage, apropos of almost *nothing*, in ultimate conflicts about *everything*. This all-*and*-nothing logic gives the interlocutors the choice, at every moment, of total incomprehension, which reduces the opposing discourse to absurdity by reducing it to its apparent logic (in this case, tomorrow's weather), or the equally total comprehension which is the tacit condition of the argument through innuendo and also of reconciliation.

'There wasn't the slightest possible chance that they could go to the Lighthouse tomorrow, Mr Ramsay snapped out irascibly.

How did he know? she asked. The wind often changed. ·

36   Ibid., p. 123.
37   It has often been observed that women fulfil a cathartic and quasi-therapeutic function of regulating men's emotional lives, calming their anger, helping them to accept the injustices and difficulties of life (cf. N. M. Henley, *Body Politics: Power, Sex and Non-verbal Communication* (Englewood Cliffs, N.J.: Prentice Hall, 1977), p. 85).

The extraordinary irrationality of her remark, the folly of women's minds enraged him. He had ridden through the valley of death, been shattered and shivered; and now she flew in the face of facts, made his children hope what was utterly out of the question, *in effect, told lies.* He stamped his foot on the stone step. "Damn you," he said. *But what had she said? Simply* that it might be fine tomorrow. So it might.
Not with the barometer falling and the wind due west.'[38]

It is because she is a woman that Mrs Ramsay has the extraordinary perspicacity that means that when she witnesses one of those pointlessly serious debates between men about cubes and squares, Voltaire and Madame de Staël, the character of Napoleon or the French system of land tenure, 'her eyes were so clear that they seemed to go round the table unveiling each of these people.'[39] Being an outsider to men's games and the obsessive exaltation of the self and the social drives they impose, she sees quite naturally that the seemingly purest and most passionate arguments for or against Walter Scott often spring from nothing more than the desire to 'put oneself forward' (another of those fundamental movements of the body, akin to the Kabyle *qabel*), as in the case of Tansley, another incarnation of masculine egotism: 'and so it would always be with him till he got his Professorship or married his wife, and so need not always be saying "I – I – I." For that was what his criticism of poor Sir Walter, or perhaps it was Jane Austen, amounted to. "I – I – I." He was thinking of himself and the impression he was making, as she could tell from the sound of his voice, and his emphasis and his uneasiness. Success would be good for him.'[40]
In fact, women are rarely so free of all dependence, if not on social games, at least on the men who play them, that they can carry disenchantment as far as this kind of somewhat condescending pity for the male *illusio*. Their whole upbringing prepares them rather to enter the game *vicariously*, that is, in a position that is both external and subordinate, and, like Mrs Ramsay, to grant masculine *concern* a kind of tender attention and confident comprehension, which *also* generate a profound

38   *To the Lighthouse*, pp. 37–8 (my italics).
39   Ibid., pp. 122–3.
40   Ibid., p. 122.

security.[41] Excluded from the games of power, they are prepared to take part in them through the men who are engaged
in them, whether it be their husband or, as in Mrs Ramsay's
case, their son: '. . . his mother, watching him guide his scissors
neatly round the refrigerator, imagined him all red and ermine
on the Bench given to or directing a stern and momentous
enterprise in some crisis of public affairs.'[42]

The principle of these affective dispositions lies in the status
given to women in the division of labour of domination: 'Just
as it is not woman's role to go to war,' says Kant, 'so she cannot
personally defend her rights and engage in civil affairs for
herself, but only through a *representative*.'[43] Renunciation,
which Kant ascribes to the female nature, is inscribed at the
deepest level of the dispositions constituting the habitus, a
second nature which never looks more like nature than when
the socially instituted *libido* is realized in a particular form of
libido, in the ordinary sense of desire. Because differential socialization disposes men to love the games of power and women
to love the men who play them, masculine charisma is partly
the charm of power, the seduction that the possession of power
exerts, as such, on bodies whose drives and desires are themselves politically socialized.[44] Masculine domination finds one

41   A number of surveys have shown that women tend to measure their own
success by that of their husband.
42   *To the Lighthouse*, p. 6.
43   Clearly Otto Weininger was not entirely wrong in claiming to speak
for Kantian philosophy when, having reproached women for their readi-
ness to adopt their husband's name, he concluded that 'woman is essentially
nameless, because she intrinsically lacks personality.' In the subsequent
text, through an association of the social unconscious, Kant moves from
women to the 'masses' (traditionally regarded as feminine) and from the
renunciation implied in the need to delegate to the 'docility' which leads
peoples to abdicate in favour of 'the fathers of their country' (I. Kant, *Anthropology from a Pragmatic Point of View* (The Hague: Martinus Nijhoff, 1974),
p. 80).
44   This point is made against the tendency to classify all the sexual
exchanges of the bureaucratic universe, particularly between managers
and secretaries (cf. R. Pringle, *Secretaries Talk: Sexuality, Power and Work*
(London and New York: Allen and Unwin, 1988), esp. pp. 84–103), either as
'sexual harassment' (which is probably still underestimated even by the most
'radical' denunciations), or as the cynical, instrumental use of female charm
as a means of access to power (cf. J. Pinto, 'Une relation enchantée: la secré-
taire et son patron', *Actes de la Recherche en Sciences Sociales*, no. 84 (1990),
pp. 32–48).

of its strongest supports in the misrecognition which results from the application to the dominant of categories engendered in the very relationship of domination and which can lead to that extreme form of *amor fati*, love of the dominant and of his domination, a *libido dominantis* (desire for the dominant) which implies renunciation of personal exercise of *libido dominandi* (the desire to dominate).

—— 3 ——
Permanence and change

It took all the insight of Virginia Woolf and the infinite refinement of her writing to pursue the analysis into the best-concealed effects of a form of domination which is inscribed in the whole social order and operates in the obscurity of bodies, which are both the stakes and the principles of its efficacy. And perhaps it was also necessary to invoke the authority of the author of *A Room of One's Own* to lend some credibility to the recalling of the hidden constants of the relation of sexual domination – so strong are the factors which, beyond simple blindness, incline people to ignore those constants (such as the legitimate pride of a feminist movement that is led to stress the advances won by its struggles).

It is indeed astonishing to observe the extraordinary autonomy of sexual structures relative to economic structures, of modes of reproduction relative to modes of production. The same system of classificatory schemes is found, in its essential features, through the centuries and across economic and social differences, at the two extremes of the space of anthropological possibles, among the highland peasants of Kabylia and among the upper-class denizens of Bloomsbury; and researchers, almost always schooled in psychoanalysis, discover, in the psychic experience of the men and women of today, processes, for the most part very deeply buried, which, like the work needed to separate the boy from his mother or the symbolic effects of the sexual division of tasks and times in production and reproduction, are seen in the full light of day in ritual practices, which are publicly and collectively performed and are integrated into the symbolic system of a society organized through and through according to the principle of the primacy of masculinity. How can we explain why the uncompromisingly androcentric vision of a world in which ultra-masculine dispositions often find the conditions most favourable to their actualization in the structures of agrarian activity – organized according to the opposition between male working time and female production time[1] – and also in the logic of a fully developed economy of symbolic goods, has been able to survive the profound changes which have occurred in productive activities and in the division of labour, relegating the economy of symbolic goods to a small number of islands, surrounded by the 'icy waters of self-interest and calculation'? How do we take account of this apparent perennity, which moreover plays a considerable part in giving the appearances of a natural essence to a historical construction, without running the risk of ratifying it by inscribing it in the eternity of a nature?

The historical labour of dehistoricization

In fact, it is clear that the eternal, in history, cannot be anything other than the product of a historical labour of eternalization. It follows that, in order to escape completely from essentialism, one should not try to deny the permanences and the invariants, which are indisputably part of historical reality;[2] but, rather, one must *reconstruct the history of the historical labour of dehistoricization*, or, to put it another way, the history of the continuous

---

1 This distinction, proposed by Marx, between working periods (that is, for agrarian activity, ploughing and sowing, the tasks of men) and production periods (germination, etc.), in which the grain undergoes a purely natural process of transformation, homologous with that which occurs in the mother's womb during gestation, has its equivalent in the cycle of reproduction, with the opposition between the time of procreation, when the man plays the active and decisive role, and the time of gestation (see P. Bourdieu, *The Logic of Practice* (Cambridge: Polity, 1990), pp. 218–20).
2 To be persuaded of this, one only has to read attentively the five volumes of *L'Histoire des femmes*, edited by Georges Duby and Michèle Perrot (Paris: Plon, 1991–2).

(re)creation of the objective and subjective structures of masculine domination, which has gone on permanently so long as there have been men and women, and through which the masculine order has been continuously reproduced from age to age. In other words, a 'history of women' which brings to light, albeit despite itself, a large degree of constancy, permanence, must, if it wants to be consistent with itself, give a place, and no doubt the central place, to the *history of the agents and institutions which permanently contribute to the maintenance of these permanences, the church, the state, the educational system, etc.,* and which may vary, at different times, in their relative weights and their functions. It cannot be content, for example, to record the exclusion of women from this or that occupation, this or that branch or discipline; it must also take note of and explain the reproduction both of the hierarchies (occupational, disciplinary, etc.) and of the hierarchical dispositions which they favour and which lead women to contribute to their own exclusion from the places from which they are in any case excluded.[3]

Historical research cannot limit itself to describing the transformations over time of the condition of women, or even the relationship between the sexes in the different epochs. It must aim to establish, for each period, the state of the system of agents and institutions – family, church, state, educational system, etc., which, with different weights and different means at different times, have helped to remove the relations of masculine domination *more or less completely from history.* The true object of a history of relations between the sexes is thus the history of the successive combinations (different in the Middle Ages and in the eighteenth century, under Pétain in the early 1940s and under de Gaulle from 1945) of structural mechanisms (such as those which ensure the reproduction of the sexual division of labour) and strategies which, through institutions and individual agents, have perpetuated the structure of the relations of domination between the sexes, in the course of a very long history, and sometimes at the price of real or

3 In some of my earliest work I undertook a small part of this immense task, when I tried to show how the educational system helps to reproduce differences not only between the social categories but also between the sexes.

apparent changes. The subordination of women may be expressed in their being required to work, as in most prein-dustrial societies, or, conversely, in their exclusion from work, as was the case after the industrial revolution, with the separa-tion of work and home, a decline in the economic weight of women in the bourgeoisie, henceforward assigned by Victorian prudishness to the cult of chastity and the domestic arts of watercolours and the piano, and also, at least in countries of Catholic tradition, to the practice of religion, which became ever more exclusively female.[4]

In short, in bringing to light the transhistorical invariants of the relationship between the 'genders', historical study is obliged to take for its object the historical labour of dehistori-cization which has continuously produced and reproduced them, in other words, the constant work of *differentiation* to which men and women have never ceased to be subject and which leads them to distinguish themselves by masculinizing or feminizing themselves. In particular it should aim to describe and analyse the endlessly renewed social (re)construction of the principles of vision and division that generate 'genders' and, more broadly, the various categories of sexual practices (het-erosexual and homosexual, in particular), heterosexuality itself being socially constructed and socially constituted as the uni-versal standard of any 'normal' sexual practice, i.e. one that has been rescued from the ignominy of the 'unnatural'.[5] A genuine understanding of the changes that have occurred both in the condition of women and in relations between the sexes can, paradoxically, be expected only from an analysis of the

4   V. L. Bullough, B. Shelton and S. Slavin, *The Subordinated Sex: A History of Attitudes toward Women*, 2nd edn (Athens: University of Georgia Press, 1988).
5   We know, notably through the book by George Chauncey, *Gay New York* (New York: Basic Books, 1994), that the advent of the opposition between homosexuals and heterosexuals is very recent, and that it was perhaps only after the Second World War that heterosexuality or homosexuality became an either-or choice. Until then, many men would move from a male to a female partner; so-called 'normal' men might sleep with 'fags' so long as they limited themselves to the 'male' side of the relationship. 'Inverts', men who desired men, adopted effeminate manners and dress, which began to regress as the distinction between homosexuals and heterosexuals became more pronounced.

transformations of the mechanisms and institutions charged with ensuring the perpetuation of the order of genders.

The work of reproduction was performed, until a recent period, by three main agencies, the family, the church and the educational system, which were objectively orchestrated and had in common the fact that they acted on unconscious structures. The family undoubtedly played the most important part in the reproduction of masculine domination and the masculine vision;[6] it is here that early experience of the sexual division of labour and the legitimate representation of that division, guaranteed by law and inscribed in language, imposes itself. As for the church, pervaded by the deep-seated anti-feminism of a clergy that was quick to condemn all female offences against decency, especially in matters of attire, and was the authorized reproducer of a pessimistic vision of women and womanhood,[7] it explicitly inculcates (or used to inculcate) a familialist[8] morality, entirely dominated by patriarchal values, with, in particular, the dogma of the radical inferiority of women. In addition it acts, more indirectly, on the historical structures of the unconscious, notably through the symbolism of the sacred texts,[9] the liturgy and even religious space and time (the latter marked by the correspondence between the structure of the liturgical year and that of the farming year). In some periods, it has been able to draw on a series of ethical oppositions corresponding to a cosmological model in order to justify the hierarchy within the family, a monarchy by divine right based on the authority of

---

6   Cf. N. J. Chodorow, *The Reproduction of Mothering: Psychoanalysis and the Sociology of Gender* (Berkeley: University of California Press, 1978).

7   On the role of the church in perpetuating the pessimistic vision of women, who were seen as responsible for moral degradation, and therefore deserving to suffer to expiate all the sins of the world, see W. A. Christian, Jr, *Visionaries: The Spanish Republic and the Reign of Christ* (Berkeley: University of California Press, 1997). This expiatory ethic was also at the centre of the restoration which the Vichy government performed, arming itself with the most archaic representation of woman, while drawing support from women, like the Spanish priests who, while condemning female impurity, exploited the minor 'visionaries', who were mainly women, and their miraculous visions (cf. F. Muel-Dreyfus, *Vichy et l'Éternel féminin* (Paris: Éditions du Seuil, 1996).

8   See note 14 below (*trans.*).

9   Cf. J. Maître, *Mystique et féminité. Essai de psychanalyse sociohistorique* (Paris: Éditions du Cerf, 1997).

the father, and to impose a vision of the social world of woman's place within it through what has been called 'iconographic propaganda'.[10]

Finally, the educational system, even when it had freed itself from the grip of the church, continued to transmit the presuppositions of the patriarchal representation (based on the homology between the man/woman relationship and the adult/child relationship) and, perhaps most importantly, those that are inscribed in its own hierarchical structures, all sexually characterized, between the various schools or faculties, between the disciplines ('soft' or 'hard' – or, closer to the original mythical intuition – 'desiccating'), between specialisms, that is, between ways of being and ways of seeing, or seeing *oneself*, one's aptitudes and inclinations, in short, everything that combines to form not only social destinies but also self-images.[11] In fact the whole of learned culture, transmitted by the educational system, whether in its literary, philosophical, medical or legal variants, has never ceased, until a recent period, to convey archaic modes of thought and models (with, for example, the weight of the Aristotelian tradition, which makes man the active principle and woman the passive principle) and an official discourse on the second sex to which theologians, jurists, doctors and moralists have all contributed and which aims to restrict the autonomy of the wife, especially as regards work, on the grounds of her 'childish' and feeble nature, each period drawing on the 'treasures' of the previous one (for example, in the sixteenth century, fabliaux in the vernacular and theologi-

---

10   Cf. S. F. Matthews-Grieco, *Ange ou diablesse. La représentation de la femme au XVIe siècle* (Paris: Flammarion, 1991), esp. p. 387: 'The means of communication were always in the hands of the stronger sex: books, images and sermons were written, drawn, declaimed by men, while most women were cut off, by sheer lack of education, from written culture and knowledge' (p. 327).

11   For a specific illustration of what is implied by this perhaps somewhat abstract evocation of the specific forms that masculine domination takes within the educational institution, see Toril Moi's analysis of the representations and academic classifications through which Sartre's hold imposed itself on Simone de Beauvoir (cf. T. Moi, *Simone de Beauvoir: The Making of an Intellectual Woman* (Oxford: Blackwell, 1994), and P. Bourdieu, 'Apologie pour une femme rangée', preface to T. Moi, *Simone de Beauvoir. Conflits d'une intellectuelle* (Paris: Diderot Éditeur, 1995), pp. vi–x).

cal dissertations in Latin).[12] But it is, at the same time, as will be seen, one of the most decisive principles of change in the relations between the sexes, because of the contradictions it both contains and introduces.

To complete the catalogue of the institutional factors of the reproduction of the gender division one should also take into account the role of the *state*, which has ratified and underscored the prescriptions and proscriptions of private patriarchy with those of a *public patriarchy*, inscribed in all the institutions charged with managing and regulating the everyday existence of the domestic unit. Without reaching the extremes of paternalist, authoritarian states (such as France under Pétain or Spain under Franco), full-scale realizations of the ultra-conservative vision which makes the patriarchal family the principle and model of the social order interpreted as a *moral order*, based on the absolute pre-eminence of men over women, adults over children, and on identification of morality with the strength, courage and self-control of the body, the seat of temptations and desires,[13] modern states have inscribed all the fundamental principles of the androcentric vision in the rules defining the official status of the citizens.[14] The essential ambiguity of the state derives in part from the fact that in its very structure, with the opposition between financial ministries and spending ministries, between its paternalist, familialist, protective right hand,

---

12   Until the nineteenth century, medicine provided anatomical and physiological justifications for the status of women (especially of their reproductive role). See P. Perrot, *Le Travail des apparences, ou les transformations du corps féminin, XVIIIe–XIXe siècle* (Paris: Éditions du Seuil, 1984).

13   Cf. G. Lakoff, *Moral Politics: What Conservatives Know that Liberals Don't* (Chicago: University of Chicago Press, 1996).

14   One would need to discuss in detail the policies for the management of bodies characteristic of the various political regimes: first, authoritarian regimes, with their great military parades and vast gymnastic exhibitions, expressing the ultra-masculine philosophy of the Conservative Revolution, based on the cult of the manly soldier and male bonding, and on the heroic ethic of the ascesis of tension (cf. G. Mosse, *L'Image de l'homme. L'invention de la virilité moderne* (Paris: Abbeville, 1997) or the regressive, paternalist folklore of the Vichy government (cf. Muel-Dreyfus, *Vichy et l'Éternel féminin*); and also those of democratic regimes, with their family policies and what Rémi Lenoir calls familialism (cf. R. Lenoir, 'La famille, une affaire d'État', *Actes de la Recherche en Sciences Sociales*, no. 113 (June 1996), pp. 16–30), and also all their educational action.

and its socially oriented left hand, it reproduces the archetypal division between male and female, with women being linked to the left hand as its administrators and as the main recipients of its benefits and services.[15]

This brief review of the set of agencies which play a part in reproducing the hierarchy of the genders should make it possible to outline the programme for a historical analysis of the constancies and transformations of these agencies; this alone can provide the instruments needed to understand both the often surprising permanent features to be observed in the condition of women (and to do so without simply invoking masculine resistance or ill-will[16] or the responsibility of women themselves) and also the visible or invisible changes that have occurred in recent times.

The factors of change

The major change has doubtless been that masculine domination no longer imposes itself with the transparency of something taken for granted. Thanks, in particular, to the immense critical effort of the feminist movement, which, at least in some regions of the social space, has managed to break the circle of generalized mutual reinforcement, it now appears, in many contexts, as something to be avoided, excused or justified. The calling into question of the self-evident comes hand in hand with the substantive transformations seen in the condition of women, especially in the most advantaged social categories. There are, for example, increased access to secondary and higher education and waged work, and, through this, to the public sphere; and a degree of distancing from

15 This reminder of the function of the state as the instrument of a mediated exercise of power counters the tendency to make masculine power over women (and children) in the family the primordial site of masculine domination; the reminder of the differentiation of this function dispels the false debate, which has divided some feminists, over whether the state is oppressive or liberatory for women.

16 This factor is of course far from negligible and acts through the aggregation of individual actions both at home and at work, and also through semi-concerted symbolic actions such as those of 'the new machismo' and some critiques of 'political correctness'.

domestic tasks[17] and reproductive functions (linked to the development and generalized use of contraception and the reduction of family size), with, in particular, the postponement of marriage and procreation, reduction of the interruption of professional activity due to childbirth, and also increased divorce and a lower rate of marriage.[18]

Of all the factors of change, the most important are those that are linked to the decisive transformation of the function of the educational system in reproducing the differences between the genders, such as women's increased access to education and, consequently, to economic independence, and the transformation of family structures (resulting, in particular, from increased rates of divorce). It is true that even when the real family has changed, the inertia of habitus, and *of law*, tends to perpetuate the dominant model of family structure and, by the same token, of legitimate sexuality – heterosexual and oriented towards reproduction – in relation to which socialization and with it the transmission of the traditional principles of division were tacitly organized; but the appearance of new types of family, such as 'composite' families, and the public visibility of new (particularly homosexual) models of sexuality help to break the *doxa* and expand the space of what is possible in terms of sexuality. In addition, and in a more banal way, the increased number of working women could not fail to affect the division of household tasks and therefore the traditional male and female models,

17   An important factor of change has been the growing number of household appliances and technical devices which (in a differential way according to social position) have helped to reduce the burden of household tasks – cooking, washing, cleaning, shopping, etc. (as is shown by the fact that the amount of time devoted to domestic work has steadily declined both in Europe and in the US), whereas time devoted to child care is harder to compress (although it is more evenly shared), despite the growth of crèches and nursery schools.

18   Cf. L. W. Hoffman, 'Changes in family roles, socialization and sex differences', *American Psychologist*, 32 (1977), pp. 644–57. It is not possible to evoke, even in a few words, the set of changes that the massive entry of women to secondary and higher education has brought about, particularly in the political and religious fields, and also in the set of strongly feminized occupations. I shall simply name, as an example, the workers' movements of an entirely new type which have called themselves 'coordinations' (cf. D. Kergoat (ed.), *Les Infirmières et leur coordination, 1988–1989* (Paris: Lamarre, 1992).

which has no doubt had consequences for the acquisition of the sexually differentiated dispositions within the family. It has been observed, for example, that the daughters of working mothers have higher career aspirations and are less attached to the traditional model of a woman's role.[19]

But one of the most important changes in the status of women and one of the most decisive factors of change is undoubtedly the increased access of girls to secondary and higher education, which, together with the transformations of the structures of production (particularly the development of large public and private bureaucracies and the social technologies of management), has led to a very important modification of the position of women in the division of labour. Women are now much more strongly represented in the intellectual professions, in administration and in the various forms of sale of symbolic services – journalism, television, cinema, radio, public relations, advertising, design and decoration; and they have intensified their presence in the occupations closer to the traditional definition of female activities (teaching, social work and paramedical activities). This having been said, while female graduates have found their main career openings in intermediate middle-range occupations (middle management, technical staff, medical and social personnel), they remain practically excluded from positions of authority and responsibility, particularly in industry, finance and politics.

The changes visible in *conditions* in fact conceal permanent features in the *relative positions*: the levelling-out of the chances of access and rates of representation should not be allowed to mask the inequalities which persist in the distribution of boys and girls among the various types of schooling and therefore among possible careers. More girls than boys obtain the baccalaureate and enter higher education, but they are much less represented in the most prestigious sections: they remain considerably underrepresented in scientific sections whereas they are ever more represented in literary courses. Similarly, in vocational lycées they remain largely confined to the low-skilled specialisms traditionally regarded as 'female' (those of local government clerk or shop assistant, secretary or nurse), while other specialist courses (mechanical, electrical or electronic engineering) are

19   Hoffman, 'Changes in family roles'.

practically reserved for boys. In the medical faculties, the proportion of women declines as one moves up the hierarchy of specialisms, some of which, such as surgery, are practically closed to them, whereas others, such as pediatrics or gynaecology, are reserved for them. As can be seen, the structure is perpetuated in pairs of oppositions homologous with the traditional divisions, such as the oppositions between the Grandes Écoles and the faculties; or, within the faculties, between the law or medical faculties and the humanities faculties; or, within the humanities, between philosophy or sociology and psychology or art history. We also know that the same principle of division still applies within each discipline, assigning to men the most noble, the most synthetic and the most theoretical studies, and to women the most analytical, the most practical and the least prestigious.[20]

The same logic governs access to the various professions and to the various positions within each of them: in work as in education, the progress made by women must not conceal the corresponding progress made by men, so that, as in a handicap race, the structure of the *gaps* is maintained.[21] The most striking example of this *permanence in and through change* is the fact that positions which become feminized are either already devalued (the majority of semi-skilled workers are women or immigrants) or declining, their devaluation being intensified, in a snowball effect, by the desertion of the men which it helped to induce. Moreover, while it is true that women are found at all levels of the social space, their chances of access (and rate of representation) decline as one moves towards the rarest and most sought-after positions (so that the rate of actual and potential feminization is no doubt the best index of the relative position and value of the various occupations).[22]

20 On the difference between the sexes in philosophical choices, cf. Charles Soullié, 'Anatomie du goût philosophique', *Actes de la Recherche en Sciences Sociales*, no. 109 (Oct. 1995), pp. 3–28.
21 R. M. Lagrave, 'Une émancipation sous tutelle. Éducation et travail des femmes au XXe siècle', in G. Duby and M. Perrot (eds), *Histoire des femmes*, vol. 5: *Le XXe siècle* (Paris: Plon, 1992).
22 H. Y. Meynaud, 'L'accès au dernier cercle. La participation des femmes aux instances de pouvoir dans les entreprises', *Revue Française des Affaires Sociales*, 42, no. 1 (Jan.–Mar. 1988), pp. 67–87; 'Au cœur de l'entreprise EDF, la lente montée des électriciens dans les postes de pouvoir', *Bulletin d'Histoire de l'Électricité*, Actes de la Journée de la Femme et l'Électricité (1993).

Thus, at each level, despite the effects of hyper-selection, the formal equality between men and women tends to disguise the fact that, other things being equal, women always occupy less favoured positions. For example, while it is true that women are more and more strongly represented among the employees of central and local government, it is always the lowest and most insecure positions that are reserved for them (there is a particularly high proportion of women among non-established and part-time staff, and in local government service, for example, they occupy junior and ancillary positions as assistants and 'carers' – cleaners, canteen staff, nursery assistants, etc.).[23] The clearest indication of the uncertainties of the status granted to women in the labour market is no doubt the fact that they are always paid less than men, other things being equal, that they are appointed to lower positions with the same qualifications, and above all that they are proportionately more affected by redundancies and insecurity of employment and more often relegated to part-time posts – which has the effect, among other things, of almost invariably excluding them from access to decision-making and career prospects.[24] Given that their interests are bound up with the 'left hand' of the state and with 'social' positions within the bureaucratic field as well as with those sectors of private companies which are most vulnerable to 'flexible labour' policies, there is every reason to expect that they will be the main victims of the neoliberal policy aimed at reducing the welfare role of the state and favouring the 'deregulation' of the labour market.

The dominant positions, which they occupy in increasing numbers, largely lie in the dominated regions of the field of power, that is, in the domain of the production and circulation of symbolic goods (publishing, journalism, the media, teaching, etc.). These 'discriminated-against elites', as María Antonia

23 Cf. M. Amine, *Les Personnels territoriaux* (Paris: Éditions du CNFPT, 1994).
24 Cf. M. Maruani, 'Féminisation et discrimination. Évolution de l'activité féminine en France', *L'Orientation Scolaire et Professionnelle*, 20, no. 3 (1991), pp. 243–56; 'Le mi-temps ou la porte', *Le Monde des Débats*, 1 (Oct. 1992), pp. 8–9; 'Statut social et mode d'emploi', *Revue Française de Sociologie*, 30 (1989), pp. 31–9; J. Laufer and A. Fouquet, 'Effet de plafonnement de carrière des femmes cadres et accès à la décision dans la sphère économique', *Rapport du Centre d'Études de l'Emploi*, 97/90.

García de León calls them, have to pay for their 'elect' positions with a constant effort to satisfy the additional demands that are almost always placed on them and to banish all sexual connotation from their bodily *hexis* and their dress.[25]

For a full understanding of the statistical distribution of powers and privileges between men and women and the way it has changed over time, one has to bear in mind, simultaneously, two properties which may at first sight appear contradictory. On the one hand, whatever their position in the social space, women have in common the fact that they are *separated from men by a negative symbolic coefficient* which, like skin colour for blacks, or any other sign of membership of a stigmatized group, negatively affects everything that they are and do, and which is the source of a systematic set of homologous differences: despite the vast distance between them, there is something in common between a woman managing director who needs a massage every morning to give her the strength to cope with the stress of exercising power over men – or among men – and the woman production-line worker in the metal industry who has to look to the solidarity of her female workmates for support against the ordeals of work in a male environment, such as sexual harassment, or, quite simply, the damage done to her self-image and self-esteem by the ugliness and dirt imposed by her working conditions. On the other hand, despite the specific experiences which bring them together (such as the small change of domination received in the countless, often subliminal, wounds inflicted by the masculine order), women remain *separated from each other* by economic and cultural differences which affect, among other things, their objective and subjective ways of undergoing and suffering masculine domination – without, however, cancelling out all that is linked to the diminution of symbolic capital entailed by being a woman.

For the rest, even the changes in the condition of women always obey the logic of the traditional model of the division between male and female. Men continue to dominate the public space and the field of power (especially economic power – over production) whereas women remain (predominantly)

25 Meynaud, 'L'accès au dernier cercle'.

assigned to the private space (domestic space, the site of reproduction), where the logic of the economy of symbolic goods is
perpetuated, or to those quasi-extensions of the domestic space,
the welfare services (especially medical services) and education,
or to the domains of symbolic production (the literary, artistic
or journalistic fields, etc.).

If the old structures of the sexual division seem still to determine the very direction and form of these changes, this is
because, as well as being objectified in disciplines, careers and
jobs that are more or less strongly characterized sexually, they
act through *three practical principles* which women, and also
their social circles, apply in their choices. The first is that the
functions appropriate to women are an extension of their
domestic functions – education, care and service.[26] The second
is that a woman cannot have authority over men, and, other
things being equal, therefore has every likelihood of being
passed over in favour of a man for a position of authority and
of being confined to subordinate and ancillary functions. The
third principle gives men the monopoly of the handling of technical objects and machines.

Questioning adolescent girls about their experience at school, one
cannot fail to be struck by the weight of the positive or negative
incitements and injunctions of parents, teachers (especially careers
advisers) and fellow pupils, who are always quick to remind them
tacitly or explicitly of the destiny assigned to them by the traditional
principle of division: thus, many of them observe that science teachers encourage girls less than boys and that parents, like teachers and
advisers, direct them 'in their own interest' away from certain careers
regarded as masculine ('When your father says "You'll never be able
to do that job", it's really annoying'), whereas they encourage their
brothers to choose them. But these reminders owe a large part of their
efficacy to the fact that a whole series of previous experiences, particularly in sport, which often gives rise to experience of discrimination, has prepared them to accept such suggestions as foreshadowings

26   In a league table of 335 occupations according to the percentage of their
members who are women, the top-ranking female jobs involve provision of
services to children (child care and teaching), the sick (nurses, dieticians),
households (cleaners and servants) and persons (secretaries, receptionists and
'bureaucratic domesticity') (see B. R. Bergman, *The Economic Emergence of
Work* (New York: Basic Books, 1986), pp. 317ff.).

and has made them internalize the dominant vision: they 'cannot see themselves giving orders to men', or, quite simply, working in a typically male occupation. The sexual division of tasks, inscribed in the objectivity of directly visible social categories, and the spontaneous interpretation of statistics which shapes the representation that each of us has of what is *normal*, have taught them that, as one of them put it in one of those wonderful tautologies in which the socially self-evident expresses itself: 'These days, you don't see many women in men's jobs.'

In short, through the experience of a 'sexually' ordered social order and the explicit reminders addressed to them by their parents, teachers and peers, themselves endowed with principles of vision acquired in similar experiences of the world, girls internalize, in the form of schemes of perception and appreciation not readily accessible to consciousness, the principles of the dominant vision which lead them to find the social order, such as it is, normal or even natural and in a sense to anticipate their destiny, refusing the courses or careers from which they are anyway excluded and rushing towards those for which they are in any case destined. The constancy of habitus that results from this is thus one of the most important factors in the relative constancy of the structure of the sexual division of labour: because these principles are, in their essentials, transmitted from body to body, below the level of consciousness and discourse, to a large extent they are beyond the grip of conscious control and therefore not amenable to transformations or corrections (as is shown by the frequently observed discrepancies between declarations and practices – for example, those men most favourable to equality between the sexes make no greater contribution to housework than others); moreover, being objectively orchestrated, they confirm and reinforce one another.

Furthermore, while refraining from attributing to men organized strategies of resistance, one can assume that the spontaneous logic of cooption, which always tends to conserve the rarest properties of social bodies, in the forefront of which is their sex ratio,[27] is rooted in a confused, and emotionally very

27 Sometimes fairly 'miraculously', as in the case of the recruitment of junior higher-education teachers which was carried out in France to cope with the influx of students (see P. Bourdieu, *Homo Academicus* (Cambridge: Polity, 1996), pp. 120–58, esp. pp. 137–9).

charged, apprehension of the threat that feminization poses for the rarity, and therefore the value, of a social position, and also, in some way, to the sexual identity of its occupants. The violence of some emotional reactions to the entry of women into a given occupation can be understood when one knows that social positions themselves are sexually characterized, and characterizing, and that, in defending their jobs against feminization, men are trying to protect their most deep-rooted idea of themselves as men, especially in the case of social categories such as manual workers or occupations such as those of the army, which owe much, if not all of their value, even in their own eyes, to their image of manliness.[28]

The economy of symbolic goods and reproduction strategies

But another decisive factor in the perpetuation of differences is the permanence that the economy of symbolic goods (of which marriage is a central component) owes to its relative autonomy, which enables masculine domination to perpetuate itself within it unaffected by the transformations of the economic modes of production – and to do so aided by the constant, explicit support that the family, the guardian of symbolic capital, receives from the churches and from law. The legitimate exercise of sexuality, although it may appear increasingly freed from the matrimonial obligation, remains ordered by and subordinated to the transmission of the patrimony, through marriage, which remains one of the legitimate routes for the transfer of wealth. As Robert A. Nye endeavours to show, bourgeois families have not ceased to invest in reproduction strategies, especially matrimonial ones, aimed at conserving or increasing their symbolic capital. They do so much more than the aristocratic families of the ancien régime, because the maintenance of their position depends strongly on the reproduction

---

28　Cf. C. L. Williams, *Gender Differences at Work: Women and Men in Nontraditional Occupations* (Berkeley: University of California Press, 1989); and M. Maruani and C. Nicole, *Au labeur des dames. Métiers masculins, emplois féminins* (Paris: Syros/Alternatives, 1989).

of their symbolic capital through the production of inheritors capable of perpetuating the heritage of the group and through the acquisition of prestigious allies;[29] and if, in modern France, the dispositions of the masculine point of honour have continued to regulate men's public activities, from duelling to etiquette or sport, this is because, as in Kabyle society, they did no more than manifest and realize the tendency of the (bourgeois) family to perpetuate itself through the reproduction strategies imposed by the logic of the economy of symbolic goods, which, especially in the universe of the domestic economy, has maintained its specific demands, distinct from those which govern the overtly economic economy of the world of business.

Being excluded from the universe of serious things, of public and especially economic affairs, women long remained confined to the domestic universe and the activities associated with the biological and social reproduction of the lineage. Even if these activities (especially the maternal ones) are apparently recognized and sometimes ritually celebrated, they are so only in so far as they remain subordinated to the activities of production, which alone receive a true economic and social sanction, and ordered in relation to the material and symbolic interests of the lineage, that is, of the men. Thus, a very large part of the *domestic work* which falls to women is, in many milieux, aimed at conserving the solidarity and integration of the family by maintaining kin relationships and all the social capital through the organization of a whole series of social activities – ordinary ones, such as meals which bring together the whole family,[30] or extra-ordinary, such as the ceremonies and celebrations (birthdays, etc.) designed to ritually celebrate the bonds of kinship and to ensure the maintenance of social relations and the prestige of the family, the exchanges of gifts, visits, letters or postcards and telephone calls.[31]

29   R. A. Nye, *Masculinity and Male Codes of Honor in Modern France* (New York: Oxford University Press, 1993), p. 9.
30   We have seen the central role of meals in family life as organized by Mrs Ramsay, the incarnation of 'family spirit', whose death leads to the collapse of the collective life and unity of the household.
31   In the case of the bourgeoisie and petite bourgeoisie of the United States, this work of maintaining the family's social capital, and therefore its unity, falls almost exclusively to the woman, who even looks after relationships with

This domestic work remains largely unnoticed or deprecated (with, for example, the ritual denunciation of women's taste for chatter, especially on the telephone . . .) and, when it is noticed, it is derealized by the transfer on to the terrain of spirituality, morality or feeling, which its non-profit-making and 'disinterested' character facilitates. The fact that women's domestic labour has no monetary equivalent does indeed help to devalue it, even in their own eyes, as if this time without a market value were also without importance and could be given without recompense, and without limits, first to the members of the family, and especially the children (thus it has been observed that a mother's time is more easily interrupted), but also outside it, for voluntary tasks, in the church or in charitable organizations, or, increasingly, in associations or political parties. Because they are often confined to unpaid activities and are therefore little inclined to reckon in terms of the monetary value of labour, women are, much more often than men, disposed towards *voluntary work*, particularly of a charitable or religious character.

Just as, in the least differentiated societies, women were treated as means of exchange enabling men to accumulate social and symbolic capital through marriages, which functioned as investments leading to the creation of more or less extensive and prestigious alliances, so too today they make a decisive *contribution* to the production and reproduction of the symbolic capital of the family, firstly by manifesting the symbolic capital of the domestic group through everything that contributes to their appearance (cosmetics, clothing, bearing, etc.); by virtue of this, they are situated on the side of appear-

---

her husband's relatives (cf. M. di Leonardo, 'The female world of cards and holidays: women, families and the world of kinship', *Signs*, 12 (Spring 1987), pp. 410–53; and, on the decisive role of telephone conversations in this work, C. S. Fischer, 'Gender and the residential telephone, 1890–1940: techniques of sociability', *Sociological Forum*, 3, no. 2 (Spring 1988), pp. 211–33). (I cannot avoid seeing an effect of submission to the dominant models in the fact that, both in France and in the United States, attention and discussion focus on a few female theorists, capable of excelling in what one of their critics has called 'the race for theory', rather than on magnificent studies, such as those just cited, which are infinitely richer and more fertile, even from a theoretical point of view, but are less in conformity with the – typically masculine – idea of 'grand theory'.)

ances and charm.[32] The social world functions (to a greater or lesser extent, depending on the field) as a market in symbolic goods, dominated by the masculine vision: for women, as has been noted, to be is to be perceived, and perceived by the male eye or by an eye informed by masculine categories – those that one implements, without being able to state them explicitly, when one praises a woman's work as 'feminine' or, on the contrary, 'not at all feminine'. To be 'feminine' means essentially to avoid all the properties and practices that can function as signs of manliness, and to say of a woman in a position of power that she is 'very feminine' is just a particularly subtle way of denying her the right to the specifically masculine attribute of power.

The particular position of women in the symbolic goods market explains the greater part of female dispositions: if every social relationship is, in one respect, the site of an exchange in which each participant invites the other to evaluate his or her perceptible appearance, then in this being-perceived, the proportion which pertains to the body reduced to what is sometimes called (potentially sexualized) 'physique', relative to less directly perceptible properties, such as speech, is greater for women than for men. Whereas, for men, cosmesis and clothing tend to efface the body in favour of social signs of social position (dress, decorations, uniform, etc.), in women they tend to highlight it and make it a language of seduction. This explains why the investment (in time, money, effort, etc.) in cosmetic work is much greater for women.

Being thus socially inclined to treat themselves as aesthetic objects and, consequently, to pay constant attention to everything concerned with beauty, the elegance of the body, its attire and its bearing, within the division of domestic labour women quite naturally take charge of everything concerned with aesthetics, and more generally with the management of the public

32 Just one index, which may appear insignificant, of the differential position of men and women in the relations of production of symbolic capital: in the US, upper-class families tend to give French first names to their daughters, who are seen as objects of fashion and seduction, whereas the boys, the guardians of the lineage and the subjects of acts designed to perpetuate it, are more likely to be given first names drawn from the stock of old names preserved by the lineage.

image and social appearances of the members of the domestic unit – the children, of course, but also the husband, who often delegates his choice of clothing to his wife. It is also women who see to and look after the décor of everyday life, the house and its internal decoration, the element of gratuitousness and 'purposefulness without purpose' which always finds a place there, even among the most deprived (just as peasants' kitchen gardens always had a corner reserved for ornamental flowers, so the meanest apartments in working-class estates have their vases of flowers, their knick-knacks and their pictures on the wall).

Being assigned to the management of the symbolic capital of the family, women are quite logically called upon to transport this role into the company, which almost always asks them to provide the functions of presentation and representation, reception and hospitality ('air hostess', 'exhibition hostess', 'conference hostess', 'receptionist', 'courier', etc.), and also the management of the major bureaucratic rituals which, like domestic rituals, help to maintain and enhance the social capital of relationships and the symbolic capital of the company.

The *extreme limit* of all the kinds of symbolic services that the bureaucratic universe asks of women is found in the luxurious Japanese hostess clubs to which big companies like to invite their executives. Unlike ordinary pleasure palaces, they purvey not sexual services but highly personalized symbolic services, such as allusions to details of the clients' personal lives and admiring references to their profession or their character. The higher the position of the club in the hierarchy of prestige and prices, the more personalized, and desexualized, are the services, tending to take on the appearances of a perfectly gratuitous gift of self, done for love and not for money, at the cost of a specifically cultural labour of euphemization (the same that is required in hotel-based prostitution, which prostitutes describe as infinitely more taxing and burdensome than the perfunctory sexual exchanges of street prostitution[33]). The profusion of personal attention and artifices of seduction, not the least of which is refined conversation which may imply a degree of erotic provocation, aims to induce in clients who must not see themselves as clients the sense

33   Cf. C. Hoigard and L. Finstad, *Prostitution, Money and Love* (Cambridge: Polity, 1992).

of being appreciated, admired, almost even desired or loved, for themselves, for their own individual person and not for their money, and of being very important, or, more simply, of 'feeling they are men'.[34]

It goes without saying that these symbolic trading activities, which are to companies what strategies of self-presentation are to individuals, demand, for their successful performance, an extreme attention to physical appearance and dispositions towards seduction which correspond to the role most traditionally assigned to women. And it is understandable that, in a general way, by a simple extension of their traditional role, women can be entrusted with functions (generally subordinate ones, although the cultural sector is one of the few in which they can occupy leading positions) in the production or consumption of symbolic goods and services, or, more precisely, of *signs of distinction*, from cosmetic products or services (hairdressers, beauticians, manicurists, etc.) to haute couture or high culture. Being responsible for the conversion of economic capital into symbolic capital within the domestic unit, they are predisposed to enter into the permanent dialectic of pretension and distinction for which fashion offers one of the most favourable terrains and which is the motor of cultural life as a perpetual movement of overtaking and outflanking. The women of the petite bourgeoisie, who go to extremes in their attention to the care of the body or cosmesis,[35] and more generally in their concern for ethical and aesthetic respectability, are the greatest victims of symbolic domination, but also the natural vectors for the relaying of its effects towards the dominated categories. Swept along by their aspiration to identify with the dominant models – as shown by their tendency towards aesthetic and linguistic hypercorrection – they are particularly inclined to appropriate at any price (which generally means on credit) the distinctive and therefore distinguished properties of the dominant classes and to contribute to their imperative popularization, in particular with the aid of

34 Cf. A. Allison, *Nightwork: Pleasure and Masculinity in a Tokyo Hostess Club* (Chicago: University of Chicago Press, 1994).
35 Cf. P. Bourdieu, *Distinction: A Social Critique of the Judgement of Taste* (Cambridge, Mass.: Harvard University Press, 1984), pp. 204–8.

the circumstantial symbolic power that their position in the apparatus of production or circulation of cultural goods (for example, in a women's magazine) may confer on their proselytizing zeal.[36] Everything therefore takes place as if the market in symbolic goods, to which women owe the most striking demonstrations of their professional emancipation, granted the appearances of freedom to these 'independent producers' only so as better to secure their eager submission and their contribution to the symbolic domination that is exercised through the mechanisms of the economy of symbolic goods, a domination of which they are also the prime victims. The awareness of these mechanisms, which is no doubt at the root of some of the strategies of subversion put forward by the feminist movement, such as the defence of the 'natural look', should extend to all the situations in which women may believe and persuade others that they exercise the responsibilities of a free agent when they are reduced to the state of instruments of symbolic exhibition or manipulation.

The strength of the structure

Thus, a truly *relational* approach to the relation of domination between men and women as it establishes itself *in the whole set of social spaces and subspaces*, that is, not only in the family but also in the educational world and the world of work, in the bureaucratic universe and in the field of the media, leads one to explode the fantastical image of the 'eternal feminine', in order to bring to light more clearly the constancy of the structure of the relation of domination between men and women which is maintained beyond the *substantive* differences in condition linked to moments in history and positions in social space. And this noting of the *transhistorical continuity of the relation of masculine domination*, far from producing an effect of dehistoricization, and therefore of naturalization, as some people sometimes pretend to believe, in fact requires one to

36 Nicole Woolsey Biggart provides an exemplary description of a paradigmatic form of cultural proselytism based on a female workforce in her book *Charismatic Capitalism* (Chicago: University of Chicago Press, 1988).

reverse the traditional problematic, based on the observation of the most visible changes in the *condition* of women. It forces us to pose the – always ignored – question of the endlessly recommenced historical labour which is necessary in order to wrench masculine domination from history and from the historical mechanisms and actions which are responsible for its apparent dehistoricization and which any politics of historical transformation needs to be aware of if it is not to be condemned to powerlessness.

Finally, and above all, it forces one to see the futility of the strident calls of 'postmodern' philosophers for the 'supersession of dualisms'. These dualisms, deeply rooted in things (structures) and in bodies, do not spring from a simple effect of verbal naming and cannot be abolished by an act of performative magic, since the genders, far from being simple 'roles' that can be played at will (in the manner of 'drag queens'), are inscribed in bodies and in a universe from which they derive their strength.[37] It is the order of genders that underlies the performative efficacy of words – and especially of insults – and it is also the order of genders that *resists* the spuriously revolutionary redefinitions of subversive voluntarism.

Like Michel Foucault, who sought to rehistoricize sexuality against psychoanalytic naturalization, by describing, in a *History of Sexuality* conceived as 'an archaeology of psychoanalysis', a genealogy of Western man as a 'subject of desire', I have tried here to link the unconscious which governs sexual relations, and, more generally, the relations between the sexes, not only to its individual ontogeny but to its collective phylogeny, in other words to the long and partly immobile history of the androcentric unconscious. But to carry through the project of understanding what it is that specifically characterizes the modern experience of sexuality, it is not sufficient, as Foucault supposed, to emphasize what differentiates it in particular from Greek or Roman antiquity in which 'one would have a difficult

---

37 Judith Butler herself seems to reject the 'voluntaristic' view of gender that she seemed to put forward in *Gender Trouble*, when she writes: 'The misapprehension about gender performativity is this: that gender is a choice, or that gender is a role, or that gender is a construction that one puts on, as one puts clothes on in the morning' (J. Butler, *Bodies that Matter: On the Discursive Limits of 'Sex'* (New York: Routledge, 1993), p. 94).

time finding . . . anything resembling the notion of "sexuality"
or "flesh" ', in other words 'a notion that refers to a single entity
and allows diverse phenomena to be grouped, despite the
apparently loose connections between them, as if they were of
the same nature . . . : behaviours, but also sensations, images,
desires, instincts, passions'.[38]

Sexuality as we understand it is indeed a historical invention,
but one which has developed progressively as the various fields
and their specific logics became differentiated. It was first necessary for the sexed (and not sexual) principle of division which
constituted the fundamental opposition of mythic reason to
cease to be applied to the whole order of the world, both physical and political, defining for example the foundations of cosmology, as it did for the pre-Socratic thinkers. The constitution
of the practices and discourses linked to sex as a separate
domain is indeed inseparable from the progressive dissociation
of mythic reason, with its polysemic, fuzzy analogies, and logical
reason, which, arising from argument within a scholastic field,
came little by little to take analogy itself for its object (with
Aristotle in particular). And the emergence of sexuality as such
is also indissociable from the appearance of a set of fields and
agents competing for the monopoly of the legitimate definition
of sexual practices and discourses – the religious field, the legal
field, the bureaucratic field – and capable of imposing that definition in practices, in particular through families and the familialist vision.

The schemes of the sexually characterized habitus are not
'fundamental structuring alternatives', as Goffman would
have it, but historical and highly differentiated structures, arising from a social space that is itself highly differentiated,
which reproduce themselves through learning processes linked
to the experience that agents have of the structures of these
spaces. Thus insertion into different fields organized according
to oppositions (strong/weak, big/small, heavy/light, fat/thin,
tense/relaxed, hard/soft, etc.) which always stand in a relation of homology with the fundamental distinction between
male and female and the secondary alternatives in which

38   M. Foucault, *The Uses of Pleasure*, vol. 2 of *The History of Sexuality*
(Harmondsworth: Viking Penguin, 1986), p. 35.

it is expressed (dominant/dominated, above/below, active-penetrating/passive-penetrated)[39] is accompanied by the inscription in the body of a series of sexually characterized oppositions which are homologous among themselves and also with the fundamental opposition.

The oppositions inscribed in the social structure of the fields serve as the support for cognitive structures, practical taxonomies, often recorded in systems of adjectives, which make it possible to produce ethical, aesthetic or cognitive judgements. For example, in the academic field there is the opposition between the temporally dominant disciplines, law and medicine, and the temporally dominated disciplines, the sciences and the humanities, and, within the latter group, between the sciences, with everything that is described as 'hard', and the humanities ('soft'), or again, between sociology, situated on the side of the agora and politics, and psychology, which is condemned to interiority, like literature.[40] Or again, in the field of power, there is the opposition, deeply scored in the objectivity of practices and properties, between industrial and commercial employers on the one hand and intellectuals on the other, and also inscribed in people's minds, in the form of explicit or implicit taxonomies which make the 'intellectual' appear, in the eyes of the 'bourgeois', as a being endowed with properties entirely situated on the side of the female – lack of realism,

39 Michel Foucault saw clearly the link between sexuality and (masculine) power, particularly in the Greek ethic, which, being made by men for men, led all sexual relations to be conceived 'in terms of the schema of penetration and male domination' (Foucault, *The Uses of Pleasure*, p. 220).
40 We know that the opposition between 'hard' and 'soft' is the form that the division of labour between the sexes takes in the domain of science – both in the division of scientific labour and in representations, the evaluation of findings, etc. In a quite different order, the literary critics of the sixteenth century opposed the solemn, masculine epic to the feminine and essentially ornamental lyric. The fundamental opposition reappears even in the field of international relations, where, relative to various other countries, the US, Britain or Germany, France occupies a position that can be described as 'feminine', as shown by the fact that in countries as different as Egypt, Greece or Japan, boys prefer to study in those countries whereas girls tend more towards France, or again that students tend to go to the US or Britain for economics, technology or law, and to France for literature, philosophy or the social sciences (cf. N. Panayotopoulos, 'Les "grandes écoles" d'un petit pays. Les études à l'étranger: le cas de la Grèce', *Actes de la Recherche en Sciences Sociales*, nos 121–2 (Mar. 1998), pp. 77–91).

otherworldliness, irresponsibility (as is clearly seen in situations in which the temporally dominant take the opportunity to call the intellectual or artist to order and, as men so often do to women, explain 'how the world works').

It follows that the genetic sociology of the sexual unconscious is logically extended into the analysis of the structures of the social universes in which this unconscious is rooted and repro- duces itself, whether it be the divisions embodied in the form of principles of division or the objective divisions that are estab- lished between social positions (and their occupants, who are preferentially male or female: doctors/nurses, employers/intel- lectuals, etc.), the most important of which, from the point of view of the perpetuation of these divisions, is undoubtedly the one which distinguishes the fields devoted to symbolic pro- duction. The fundamental opposition, of which Kabyle society offers the canonical form, is 'geared down' or diffracted in a series of homologous oppositions, which reproduce it, but in dispersed and often almost unrecognizable forms (such as sciences/humanities or surgery/dermatology). These specific oppositions channel the mind, in a more or less insidious way, without ever allowing themselves to be seen in their unity and for what they are, namely, so many facets of one and the same structure of relations of sexual domination.

It is however on condition that one holds together the total- ity of the sites and forms in which this kind of domination is exercised – a domination which has the particularity of being able to be exercised on very different scales, in all social spaces, from the most restricted, such as families, to the broadest – that it becomes possible to grasp its structural constants and the mechanisms of its reproduction. The visible changes that have affected the condition of women mask the permanence of the invisible structures, which can only be brought to light by rela- tional thinking capable of *making the connection between the domestic economy, and therefore the division of labour and powers which characterizes it, and the various sectors of the labour market* (the fields) in which men and women are involved. This is in contrast to the common tendency to consider *separately* the dis- tribution of tasks, and especially ranks, in domestic work and in non-domestic work.

The true nature of the structural relations of sexual domination can be glimpsed when one observes, for example, that
women who attain very high positions (senior executive, head
of a ministry, etc.) have to 'pay' in a sense for this professional
success with less 'success' in the domestic realm (divorce, late
marriage or no marriage, difficulties or failures with children,
etc.) and in the economy of symbolic goods, or, conversely, that
the success of the domestic undertaking is often achieved at the
price of partial or total renunciation of major professional
success (particularly through the acceptance of 'advantages'
which are made so readily available to women only because
they put them out of the race for power: half-time work, a 'four-
day week', etc.). Only when one takes account of the constraints that the structure of the (actual or potential) domestic
space brings to bear on the structure of the occupational space
(for example, through the representation of a necessary,
unavoidable, or acceptable gap between the husband's position
and the wife's) does it become possible to understand the
homology between the structures of the male positions and the
female positions in the various social spaces, a homology which
tends to be maintained even when the terms constantly change
their substantive content, in a chase in which women never
overcome their handicap.[41]

The making of this connection also enables one to understand
how the same relation of domination may be observed, in different forms, in the most contrasting social conditions, from the
voluntary devotion of the women of the grande bourgeoisie of
money and business to their homes or their charitable activities, to the ancillary and 'mercenary' devotion of domestic servants, or, in between, at the level of the petite bourgeoisie, a

41   Possession of strong cultural capital is not enough in itself to give a
woman access to the conditions of real economic and cultural autonomy with
respect to men. If we take the word of those who observe that, in a couple
in which the man earns a lot of money, the woman's work appears as an elec-
tive choice which has to be justified by additional activity and success or that
a man who brings in more than half the income expects the woman to do
more than half the domestic work, economic independence, a necessary condition, is not in itself sufficient to enable a woman to free herself from the
constraints of the dominant model, which may continue to haunt male and
female habitus.

waged job complementary to that of the husband, and compatible with it, and almost always performed in a minor mode. The structure of masculine domination is the ultimate principle of these countless singular relationships of domination/submission, which, while they differ in their form according to the position in space of the agents concerned – sometimes immense and visible, sometimes infinitesimal and almost invisible, but homologous and therefore united by a family resemblance – separate and unite men and women in each of the social universes, thus maintaining between them the 'mystic boundary' to which Virginia Woolf referred.

Postscript on domination and love

To stop at this point would be to surrender to what Virginia Woolf called 'the pleasure of disillusioning' (which is no doubt one of the satisfactions surreptitiously pursued by sociology), and to exclude from the inquiry the whole enchanted universe of relations of love.[42] This temptation is all the stronger because it is not easy, without running the risk of 'comic pedantry', to speak of love in the language of analysis, and, more precisely, to escape the dilemma of lyricism and cynicism, the fairytale and the fabliau. Is love an exception, the only one, but of the first order of magnitude, to the law of masculine domination, a suspension of symbolic violence, or is it the supreme – because the most subtle, the most invisible – form of that violence? When it takes the form of love of destiny, *amor fati*, in one or another of its variants, such as the espousal of the inevitable which used to lead many women, at least in traditional Kabylia or in the Béarn in bygone times, and no doubt far beyond (as is suggested by the statistics on homogamy), to find lovable and to love the man whom social destiny assigned to them, love is domination accepted, unrecognized as such and practically recognized, in happy or unhappy passion. And what is to be said of the investment, imposed by necessity or habituation, in the most detestable conditions of existence or the most dangerous occupations?

But Cleopatra's nose is there to remind us, with all the mythology of the maleficent power, terrifying and fascinating, of the woman of all mythologies – Eve the temptress, the seductive Omphale, the spell-binding Circe – that the mysterious grip of love can also take hold of men. The forces that are suspected of working in the darkness and secrecy of intimate relations ('pillow talk') and of binding men through the magic of the attachments of passion, making them forget the obligations

---

42   I have often mentioned, in particular at the end of *Distinction*, the role that the pursuit of the pleasures of 'lucid vision' might have in the specifically sociological *libido sciendi*, without seeing that the 'pleasure of disillusioning' that is inseparable from it might explain, and in part justify, some of the most violently negative reactions aroused by sociology.

linked to their social dignity, bring about a reversal of the
relation of domination, a deadly break in the ordinary, normal,
natural order which is condemned as an offence against nature
that can only reinforce the androcentric mythology.

But this is still a context of struggle, or war, and it excludes
the very possibility of the suspension of power relations which
seems constitutive of the experience of love or friendship. In
that seemingly miraculous truce in which domination seems
dominated, or, rather, cancelled out, and male violence stilled
(women, it has many times been established, civilize by stripping social relations of their coarseness and brutality), there is
an end to the masculine view of relations between the sexes,
based on the imagery of hunting or warfare; equally there is an
end to the strategies of domination, which aim to bind, chain,
subject, subordinate or enslave by inducing anxieties, uncertainties, expectations, frustrations, wounds and humiliations,
thereby reintroducing the dissymmetry of unequal exchange.

But, as Sasha Weitman puts it so well, the break with the
ordinary order is not achieved at a stroke, once and for all. It is
only by an endless labour, endlessly recommenced, that the
'enchanted island' of love, a closed and perfectly autarkic world
which is the site of a continuous series of miracles, can be
snatched from the icy waters of calculation, violence and self-
interest. This is a world of non-violence, made possible by the
establishment of relations based on full *reciprocity* and autho-
rizing the abandonment and entrusting of self; a world of
mutual recognition, which makes it possible, as Sartre says, to
feel 'justified in existing', accepted, even in one's most contingent or most negative particularities, in and by the arbitrary
absolutizing of the arbitrariness of an encounter ('because it was
him, because it was me'); the world of the *disinterestedness*
which makes possible deinstrumentalized relations, based on
the happiness of giving happiness,[43] of finding in the wonder-
ment of the other, especially at the wonder he or she arouses,
inexhaustible reasons for wonder. These are so many features,
brought to their highest degree, of the *economy of symbolic
exchanges*, of which the supreme form is the gift of self, and of

43   Which contrasts absolutely with instrumental treatment of others, as a
pure means of enjoyment, without regard for their *own ends*.

one's body, a sacred object, excluded from commercial circulation, and which, because they presuppose and produce durable and non-instrumental relations, are diametrically opposed, as David Schneider has shown, to the exchanges of the labour market, temporary and strictly instrumental relations between indifferent, interchangeable agents – of which venal or mercenary love, a true contradiction in terms, represents the limiting case, universally recognized as sacrilegious.[44]

'Pure love', the art for art's sake of love, is a relatively recent historical invention, as is art for art's sake, the pure love of art with which it is bound up, historically and structurally.[45] It is probably found only rarely in its most fully realized form, and, as a limit that is hardly ever attained, is extremely fragile because it is associated with excessive demands, 'follies' (is it because so much is invested in it that the 'marriage for love' has shown itself to be so prone to divorce?) and endlessly threatened by the crisis induced by the return of egoistic calculation or the simple effect of routinization. But it exists sufficiently, despite everything, especially in women, to be instituted as a norm, or as a practical ideal, worthy of being pursued for itself and for the exceptional experiences that it provides. The aura of mystery that surrounds it, especially in the literary tradition, is easy to understand *from a strictly anthropological point of view*: based on the suspension of the struggle for symbolic power that springs from the quest for recognition and the associated temptation to dominate, the mutual recognition by which each recognizes himself or herself in another whom he or she recognizes as another self and who also recognizes him or her as such, can lead, in its perfect reflexivity, beyond the alternatives of egoism and altruism and even beyond the distinction between subject and object, to the state of fusion and communion, often evoked in metaphors close to those of mysticism, in which two beings can 'lose themselves in each other' without being lost. Breaking away from the instability and insecurity characteristic of the dialectic of honour which, although based on a premise of equality, is always

44   Cf. P. Bourdieu, 'Le corps et le sacré', *Actes de la Recherche en Sciences Sociales*, 104 (Sept. 1994), p. 2.
45   Cf. P. Bourdieu, *The Rules of Art: Genesis and Structure of the Literary Field* (Cambridge: Polity, 1996).

exposed to domineering rivalry, the loving subject can obtain recognition only from another subject, but one which, like himself or herself, abdicates the intention of dominating. He or she freely hands his or her freedom to a master who in turn hands over his or her own, coinciding with him or her in an act of free alienation that is indefinitely asserted (through the non-redundant repetition of 'I love you'). He or she has the experience of being a quasi-divine creator who makes, *ex nihilo*, the beloved, through the power that she or he grants him or her (in particular the power of *naming*, manifested in all the unique and secret names that lovers give each other and which, as in an initiatory ritual, mark a new birth, an absolute first beginning, a change of ontological status); but a creator who, in return and simultaneously, unlike an egocentric and dominating Pygmalion, accepts to be the creature of his creature.

Mutual recognition, exchange of justifications for existing and reasons for being, mutual testimony of *trust* . . . so many signs of the perfect reciprocity through which the circle in which the loving dyad encloses itself, as an elementary social unit, indivisible and charged with a powerful symbolic autarky, becomes endowed with the power to rival successfully all the consecrations that are ordinarily asked of the institutions and rites of 'Society', the secular substitute for God.[46]

46   On the theologico-political function of institution and its rites, see P. Bourdieu, *Pascalian Meditations* (Cambridge: Polity, 2000), pp. 237–45.

Conclusion

When a scientific analysis of a form of domination is made publicly available, this necessarily has social effects, but they may run in two opposing directions: it may either symbolically reinforce domination, when its findings seem to confirm or intersect with the dominant discourse (whose negative verdicts often take the appearance of a pure constative recording), or help to neutralize it, rather like the revelation of a state secret, by favouring the mobilization of the victims. It is therefore exposed to all kinds of misunderstandings, easier to foresee than to dispel in advance.

Faced with such difficult conditions of reception, the analyst might be tempted simply to invoke his or her good faith if he or she did not know that, in such sensitive matters, good faith is not enough; nor, for that matter, is the activist's conviction which inspires many writings on the condition of women (and which generates interest in objects previously ignored or neglected). For one cannot overestimate the risks that arise for any scientific project that allows its object to be imposed on it by external considerations, however noble and generous they may be. 'Good causes' are no substitute for epistemological justifications and do not allow one to dispense with the reflexive analysis which sometimes leads to the discovery that the propriety of 'good intentions' does not necessarily exclude an interest in the profits associated with fighting a 'good fight' (which does not all imply that, as I have sometimes been claimed to say, 'every activist project is non-scientific'). While there is no question of trying to rid science of the individual or collective motivation aroused by the existence of political and intellectual mobilization, in the name of some kind of utopian *Wertfreiheit* ('refusal of value judgements'), the fact remains that the best of political movements will inevitably produce bad science, and, in the long run, bad politics, if it is not able to convert its subversive dispositions into a critical inspiration – critical firstly of itself.

It is understandable that, in order to avoid *ratifying* the real under the appearance of scientifically recording it, one may be led to pass over in silence the most visibly negative effects of domination and exploitation. Thus some authors, out of a concern to rehabilitate or a fear of giving weapons to the racism which precisely inscribes these cultural differences in the nature of the dominated and which 'blames the victims' by bracketing off the conditions of existence of which they are the product, take the more or less conscious decision to speak of 'popular culture' or, in connection with blacks in the United States, the 'culture of poverty'; while others, like some contemporary feminists, prefer to 'avoid the analysis of submission, for fear that admitting women's participation in the relation of domination might amount to shifting the burden of responsibility from men to women'.[1] In fact, against the apparently generous temptation, to which so many subversive movements have succumbed, to put forward an idealized representation of the oppressed and the stigmatized in the name of fellow-feeling, solidarity or moral indignation, and to pass over in silence the very effects of domination, especially the most negative ones, one has to take the risk of seeming to justify the established order by bringing to light the properties through which the dominated (women, manual workers, etc.), as domination has made them, may contribute to their own domination.[2] Appearances – I have said

1   J. Benjamin, *The Bonds of Love: Psychoanalysis, Feminism and the Problem of Domination* (New York: Pantheon Books, 1988), p. 9.
2   Similarly, to bring to light the effects that masculine domination exerts on the habitus of men does not mean, as some would like to think, trying to exculpate men. It means showing that the effort to liberate women from domination, i.e. from the objective and embodied dispositions that impose it on them, must be accompanied by an effort to free men from the same structures which lead them to help to impose it.

this many times – always support appearance, and the enterprise of unveiling is likely to incur both the indignant condemnations of conservatism and the pharisaical denunciations of revolutionarism. Thus, Catharine MacKinnon, who has good reason to be particularly lucid about the probable effects of lucidity, regrets that when she endeavours to describe the true nature of relations between the sexes, she is immediately accused of being 'condescending to women' when she is simply showing 'how women are condescended to'.[3] Such an accusation is even more likely in the case of a man, who clearly has no answer to those who invoke the absolute authority of their 'experience' of femininity to condemn without appeal any attempt to conceptualize the object of which they so easily claim a monopoly.[4]

This having been said, the prejudice often encountered by men's writing on sexual difference is not always without foundation. This is not only because the analyst, who is caught up in what he thinks he is comprehending, may, unwittingly following justificatory intentions, present the presuppositions that he has himself brought in as revelations as to the presuppositions of the agents. It is also, and more importantly, because, dealing with an institution that has been inscribed for millennia in the objectivity of social structures and in the subjectivity of cognitive structures, and therefore having at his disposal in order to conceptualize the opposition between male and female only a mind structured according to that opposition, he is liable to use as instruments of knowledge schemes of perception and thought which he ought to treat as objects of knowledge. And so even the most alert of analysts (Kant, Sartre, Freud, even Lacan . . .) is liable to draw unwittingly on an

---

3   C. A. MacKinnon, *Feminism Unmodified: Discourses on Life and Law* (Cambridge, Mass.: Harvard University Press, 1987).
4   To claim the monopoly of any object (if only by simple use of the 'we' that is common in some feminist writings), on the grounds of the cognitive privilege that is presumed to be granted by the mere fact of being both subject and object, and more precisely of having first-person experience of the singular form of the human condition that is to be scientifically analysed, is to bring into the scientific field the political defence of particularisms which justifies *a priori* suspicion, and to call into question the universalism which, especially through the right of access of all to all objects, is one of the foundations of the Republic of science.

unthought unconscious for the instruments of thought that he uses in order to think the unconscious.

And so, if, after much hesitation and with much trepidation, I have ventured on to an extremely difficult terrain, currently occupied almost exclusively by women, it is because I felt that the relationship of sympathetic externality in which I found myself might enable me to produce, with the aid of the immense body of work encouraged by the feminist movement, and also of the findings of my own research on the social causes and effects of symbolic domination, an analysis capable of giving a different orientation both to research on the condition of women, or, to speak more relationally, on relations between the sexes, and to the action aimed at changing those relations. For it seems to me that, while the domestic unit is one of the sites where masculine domination manifests itself most indisputably and most visibly (and not only through recourse to physical violence), the principle of the perpetuation of the material and symbolic power relations exerted there is largely situated outside that unit, in agencies such as the church, the educational system or the state, and in their strictly political actions, whether overt or hidden, official or unofficial (to be persuaded of this, one only has to observe the reactions and resistance to the current proposal for a 'contrat d'union civile'[5]).

Thus, while the feminist movement has made a major contribution to a considerable enlargement of the area of what is political or can be politicized, by making it possible to discuss or challenge politically objects and preoccupations excluded or ignored by the political tradition because they seem to belong to the private domain, it should not let itself be led to exclude, on the grounds that they belong to the most traditional logic of politics, struggles over agencies which, through their negative and (because they are attuned to the structures of the male and also female unconscious) largely invisible action, make a significant contribution to the perpetuation of the social relations of domination between the sexes. But equally it should not let itself be confined within forms of struggles that are

---

5 A 'contract of civil union' giving homosexual couples a status analogous to that of a married heterosexual couple (*trans.*).

conventionally labelled feminist, such as the demand for parity between men and women within political organizations. While they have the merit of showing that the theoretical universalism flaunted by constitutional law is not always as universal as it seems – especially in as much as it recognizes only abstract individuals, devoid of social qualities – these struggles are liable to reinforce the effects of another form of fictitious universalism, by favouring firstly women drawn from the same regions of social space as the men who currently occupy the dominant positions.

Only political action that really takes account of all the effects of domination that are exerted through the objective complicity between the structures embodied in both women and men and the structures of the major institutions through which not only the masculine order but the whole social order is enacted and reproduced (starting with the state, structured around the opposition between its male 'right hand' and its female 'left hand', and the educational system, responsible for the effective reproduction of all the principles of vision and division, and itself organized around analogous oppositions) will be able, no doubt in the long term and with the aid of the contradictions inherent in the various mechanisms or institutions concerned, to contribute to the progressive withering away of masculine domination.

—— Appendix ——
Some questions on the gay and lesbian movement

The gay and lesbian movement, both tacitly, by its existence and its symbolic actions, and explicitly, by the discourses and theories that it produces or to which it gives rise, raises a number of questions which are among the most important ones in the social sciences, and, in some cases, entirely new.[1] This movement of revolt against a particular form of symbolic violence, as well as bringing into existence new objects of analysis, very profoundly calls into question the prevailing symbolic order and poses in an entirely radical way the question of the foundations of that order and the conditions for a successful mobilization with a view to subverting it.

The particular form of symbolic domination suffered by homosexuals, who are marked by a stigma which, unlike skin colour or female gender, can be concealed (or flaunted), is imposed through collective acts of categorization which set up significant negatively marked differences, and so create groups – stigmatized social categories. As in some kinds of racism, this

---

1   In this text, of which I presented a first sketch at a meeting devoted to research on gays and lesbians, I shall refer only to 'the movement', without taking a position on the very complex relationship that the various groups – collectives and associations – that constitute it have with the 'collectivity/ies' or 'category/ies' – rather than 'community/ies' – of gays or lesbians, which are themselves very difficult to define (should the criterion be sexual practices – and then, declared or hidden, actual or potential? – frequenting certain places, a certain lifestyle, etc.?).

symbolic domination takes the form of a denial of public, visible existence. Oppression in the form of 'invisibilization' comes through a refusal of legitimate, public existence, i.e. of an existence that is known and recognized, especially by law, and through a stigmatization which never appears more clearly than when the movement claims visibility. It is then explicitly invited to return to the 'discretion' or dissimulation that it is ordinarily required to observe.

To speak of domination or symbolic violence is to say that, except in the case of a subversive revolt leading to inversion of the categories of perception and appreciation, the dominated tend to adopt the dominant point of view on themselves. Especially through the *destiny effect* produced by stigmatizing categorization and in particular through real or potential insults, they can thus be led to apply to themselves and accept, under constraint, 'straight' categories of perception ('straight' as opposed to 'crooked', bent, as in the Mediterranean vision), and to feel ashamed of the sexual experience which, from the point of view of the dominant categories, defines them, oscillating between the fear of being perceived, unmasked, and the desire to be recognized by other homosexuals.

The particularity of this relationship of symbolic domination is that it is linked not to visible sexual signs but to sexual practice. The dominant definition of the legitimate form of this practice as the relation of dominance of the masculine principle (active, penetrating) over the female principle (passive, penetrated) implies the taboo of the sacrilegious feminization of the masculine, i.e. of the dominant principle, which is inscribed in the homosexual relationship. Bearing witness to the universality of the recognition granted to the androcentric mythology, gays themselves very often apply the dominant principles to themselves, even though, together with women, they are the prime victims of those principles. In the couples that they form, they often reproduce, as do lesbians, a division of male and female roles that does not tend to bring them closer to the feminists (who are always ready to suspect their complicity with the male gender to which they belong, even if it oppresses them), and they sometimes take to extremes the affirmation of manliness in its commonest form, no doubt in reaction against the once dominant 'effeminate' style.

Inscribed both in objectivity, in the form of instituted divisions, and in bodies, in the form of an internalized relation of domination (revealed in shame), the parallel oppositions which are constitutive of this mythology structure the perception of one's own body and of the uses, especially the sexual ones, that are made of it, i.e. both the sexual division of labour and the division of sexual labour. And it is perhaps because it recalls in a particularly acute way the link between sexuality and power, and therefore politics (for example, by evoking the doubly 'unnatural' and therefore monstrous character that passive homosexuality with a dominated agent takes on in many societies), that analysis of homosexuality can lead to a *politics* (or a *utopia*) *of sexuality* aimed at radically differentiating the sexual relation from a power relation.

But in the absence of the will or the capacity to undertake such a radical subversion of the social structures and the cognitive structures which would have to mobilize all the victims of a sexually based discrimination (and, more generally, all those who are stigmatized), one is inevitably trapped in one of the most tragic antinomies of symbolic domination: how can people revolt against a socially imposed categorization except by organizing themselves as a category constructed according to that categorization, and so implementing the classifications and restrictions that it seeks to resist (rather than, for example, fighting for a new sexual order in which the distinction between the different sexual statuses would be indifferent)? Can the movement which has helped to underline the fact that, like the family, the region or any other collective entity, the status of gay or lesbian is nothing but a social construction, based on belief, be satisfied with the symbolic revolution capable of making that construction visible, known and recognized, of conferring on it the full and complete existence of a *realized category* by inverting the sign of the stigma and making it an emblem – like 'gay pride', the public, momentary, extraordinary manifestation of the collective existence of the invisible group? All the more so since, by revealing the status of 'gay' or 'lesbian' to be a social construction, a collective fiction of the 'heteronormative' order, *which has moreover partly been constructed against the homosexual,* and by underlining the extreme diversity of all the members of that constructed category, the movement tends (and this is another antinomy) in a sense to dissolve its own social bases, the very ones that it has to construct in order to exist as a social force capable of overthrowing the dominant symbolic order and in order to give strength to the demand of which it is the bearer.

And should it push its demands (and its contradiction) to their logical conclusion by asking the state to give the stigmatized group the durable and ordinary recognition of a public, published status, in a solemn act of registration? For it is true that the action of symbolic subversion, if it wants to be realistic, cannot draw the line at symbolic breaks – even if, like some aesthetic provocations, they are effective in suspending self-evidences. To accomplish a durable change in representations, it must perform and impose a durable transformation of the internalized categories (schemes of thought) which, through upbringing and education, confer the status of self-evident, necessary, undisputed natural reality, within the scope of their validity, on the social categories that they produce. It must ask law for a recognition of the particularity which implies its annulment: for everything takes place as if the homosexuals who have had to fight to move from invisibility to visibility, to cease to be excluded and made invisible, sought to become invisible again, and in a sense neutered and neutralized by submission to the dominant norm.[2] And one only has to consider all the contradictions implied in the notion of 'head of the household' when it is applied to one of the members of a homosexual couple to understand that the realism that leads people to see the 'contract of civil union' as the price to be paid for 'acceptance' and for the right to the *visible invisibility* of the

---

2 The structural contradiction that is at their heart condemns movements springing from dominated and stigmatized groups to oscillate between invisibilization and exhibition, between the suppression and the celebration of difference. As a consequence, like the Civil Rights movement and the feminist movement, they adopt one or the other strategy according to the circumstances, depending on the structure of the organizations, their access to politics and the kinds of opposition they encounter (cf. M. Bernstein, 'Celebration and suppression: the strategic uses of identity by the lesbian and gay movement', *American Journal of Sociology*, no. 103 (Nov. 1997), pp. 531–65.

good soldier, the good citizen or the good spouse, and by the same token, to a minimum share in the rights normally granted to any full member of the community (such as rights of succession), does not readily justify, for many homosexuals, the concessions to the symbolic order implied in such a contract, such as the premise of the dependent status of one member of the couple. (It is remarkable that, as Annick Prieur notes,[3] as if to minimize the inconsistency that results from maintaining difference, and even hierarchy, within couples resulting from the scandalous transgression of the sacred frontier between male and female, the associations of homosexuals in the Nordic countries that have won recognition of the civil union of homosexuals have chosen to put forward couples of quasi-twins presenting none of the signs tending to recall that division and the active/passive opposition which underlies it.)

Is it possible to convert the antinomy into a choice between alternatives amenable to a rational decision? The strength of orthodoxy, in other words the 'straight' and conservative *doxa* that every form of domination (white, male, bourgeois) imposes, is that it constitutes the particularities which result from historical discrimination as embodied dispositions invested with all the signs of naturalness. These dispositions, generally so deeply adjusted to the objective constraints of which they are the product that they imply a form of tacit acceptance of those constraints (with, for example, ghettoization as 'love of the ghetto'), inevitably appear either, when they are attached to members of the dominant groups, as unmarked, neutral, universal attributes, in other words, as both visible and distinctive and at the same time invisible, unmarked, natural ('natural distinction'), or, when they are attached to members of dominated groups, as 'differences', in other words, as shortcomings, even stigmata, requiring justification. Orthodoxy thus gives an objective basis, and a terrible efficacy, to all the strategies of the universalist hypocrisy which, reversing the responsibilities, denounces any demand for access by the dominated to common rights and status as a particularist or 'communi-

3 A. Prieur and R. S. Halvorsen, 'Le droit à l'indifférence: le mariage homosexuel', *Actes de la Recherche en Sciences Sociales*, no. 113 (1996), pp. 6–15.

tarian' breach of the universalist contract. For, paradoxically, it is when they mobilize to demand universal rights which they are in fact denied that the members of symbolic minorities are recalled to the order of the universal. The particularism and 'communitarianism' of the gay and lesbian movement are never more violently condemned than when, in particular in support of the contract of civil union, they demand that the common law be applied to gays and lesbians (who are doubly dominated, even within a movement that is made up of 90 per cent gays and 10 per cent lesbians and marked by a strongly masculinist tradition).

How, then, can one stand up to a hypocritical universalism without universalizing a particularism? In more realistic, that is to say more directly political, terms, how can one prevent the conquests of the movement from ending up as a form of ghettoization? Because it is based on a particularity of behaviour which does not imply and does not necessarily entail economic and social handicaps, the gay and lesbian movement brings together individuals who, although stigmatized, are relatively privileged, especially in terms of cultural capital, which constitutes a considerable asset in their symbolic struggles. The objective of every movement committed to symbolic subversion is to perform a labour of symbolic destruction and construction aimed at imposing new categories of perception and appreciation, so as to construct a group or, more radically, to destroy the very principle of division through which the stigmatizing group and the stigmatized group are produced. Homosexuals are particularly well armed to achieve this task and they can implement the advantages linked to particularism in the service of universalism, especially in subversive struggles.

There is a final difficulty to consider: because this movement, like the feminist movement, has the particularity of bringing together agents endowed with strong cultural capital, it is bound to encounter, in a particularly acute form, the problem of delegation to a spokesperson capable of making the group by embodying it and expressing it, and, like some movements of the far left, it tends to atomize into sects engaged in struggles for the monopoly of the public expression of the group. As a consequence, it may be that the only way for such a movement to escape a mutually reinforcing ghettoization and sectarianism is for it to place the specific capacities that it owes to the relatively improbable combination of a strong subversive disposition, linked to a stigmatized status, and strong cultural capital at the service of the social movement as a whole; or – to think in utopian terms for a moment – to place itself at the avant-garde, at least as regards theoretical work and symbolic action (in which some homosexual groups are pastmasters), of the subversive political and scientific movements, thus applying, in the service of the universal, the particular advantages which distinguish homosexuals from other stigmatized groups.

Index